THE ESSENCE OF
TAIJIQUAN PUSH-HANDS AND
FIGHTING TECHNIQUE

of related interest

Daoist Nei Gong
The Philosophical Art of Change
Damo Mitchell
Foreword by Dr Cindy Engel
ISBN 978 1 84819 065 8
eISBN 978 0 85701 033 9

XinYi WuDao
Heart-Mind—The Dao of Martial Arts
Master Zhongxian Wu
Foreword by Grandmaster Zhao ShouRong
ISBN 978 1 84819 206 5
eISBN 978 0 85701 156 5

The Mysterious Power of Xingyi Quan
A Complete Guide to History, Weapons and Fighting Skills
C S Tang
ISBN 978 1 84819 140 2
eISBN 978 0 85701 115 2

THE ESSENCE *of* TAIJIQUAN PUSH-HANDS *and* FIGHTING TECHNIQUE

WANG FENGMING

AUTHORITY: FENG ZHIQIANG

Photography and assistants in photos:
Pauli Järvelä and Wang Chao

Illustrations (excl. TCM illustrations in Chapter IV),
editing, and translation: Heikki Lindholm

SINGING
DRAGON
LONDON AND PHILADELPHIA

English language edition first published in 2015
by Singing Dragon
an imprint of Jessica Kingsley Publishers
73 Collier Street
London N1 9BE, UK
and
400 Market Street, Suite 400
Philadelphia, PA 19106, USA

www.singingdragon.com

First published in Chinese by People's Sports Publishing House, 2007–2012

Library of Congress Cataloging in Publication Data
Wang, Fengming, 1952-
  [Tai ji tui shou ji ji chuan zhen. English]
  The essence of Taijiquan push-hands and fighting technique / Master Wang Fengming.
     pages cm
  "First published in Chinese by People's Sports Publishing House, 2007-2012"--T.p. verso.
  ISBN 978-1-84819-245-4 (alk. paper)
  1. Tai chi. I. Title.
  GV504.W35 2015
  796.815--dc23
                        2014017150

British Library Cataloguing in Publication Data
A CIP catalogue record for this book is available from the British Library

ISBN 978 1 84819 245 4
eISBN 978 0 85701 190 9

Printed and bound in Great Britain by Bell and Bain Ltd, Glasgow

Publisher's Foreword

The Essence of Taijiquan Push-Hands and Fighting Technique derives from the skills passed on by the well-known ninth generation lineage holder of Chen-style Taijiquan, Grandmaster Chen Fake, and his pre-eminent disciple, Grandmaster Feng Zhiqiang, who is regarded as the "Giant of Taijiquan" by many martial artists in China and abroad. Master Wang Fengming, the author of the present work, is an internationally known Taijiquan master, an author, and a top disciple of Grandmaster Feng Zhiqiang.

This textbook is highly esteemed for the essential theories, unique techniques, and systematic and comprehensive knowledge included. The substance of the book has already been used as teaching material for push-hands and fighting technique by many martial arts academies, schools, and societies worldwide.

The original Chinese edition of this book has been reprinted many times in mainland China and was also issued in Taiwan after its publication as it was so well received by Taijiquan enthusiasts. Therefore, we would like to recommend this English translation to Taijiquan practitioners around the globe.

Contents

About the Author

Master Wang Fengming, born in Beijing in 1952, started to learn Shaolinquan at the age of eight from Master Wang Youzhi, and later Baguazhang from Master Liu Xinghan, a fourth generation master of Baguazhang. In 1975, he became a formal disciple of Grandmaster Feng Zhiqiang, a tenth generation master of Chen-style Taijiquan and also a master of Qigong, and began to learn Taijiquan, Qigong, and other traditional techniques.

Master Wang Fengming has devoted himself to the practice and study of martial arts for decades and has mastered Taijiquan, Qigong, and Baguazhang. Having achieved real *gongfu* and developed comprehensively, he is proficient in techniques and has become one of the successful disciples of Grandmaster Feng. He has won many prizes in Taijiquan and Qigong competitions at home and abroad.

Master Wang Fengming also engages in researching technical theories. His books, including *Special Taoist Taiji Stick and Ruler Qigong* and *Gem of Taoist Qigong—Inner Dan Gong and Outer Dan Gong*, in Chinese, English, and Spanish, have been well received in every corner of the world. In addition, more than a dozen of his papers and essays on Taijiquan and Qigong have been published in martial arts magazines. He also studied for three years at the Research Institute of Chinese Traditional Medicine in order to have a better understanding of the theory of Chinese traditional medicine.

In 1982 Master Wang Fengming started to teach Wushu, Taijiquan, and Qigong at the Beijing International Education Center. He acted as a coach, senior coach, coach in chief, and deputy general manager at the center. He trained many domestic and foreign students, and contributed to the popularization of Taijiquan and Qigong. At the same time, he was a qualified national-rank referee of martial arts and the Deputy Director of Zhiqiang Martial Art Academy.

Master Wang Fengming has been invited to many countries, including Canada, Finland, France, Germany, Japan, Korea, the Netherlands, Spain,

Sweden, Switzerland, the United Kingdom, and the United States, to participate in exchange activities or to teach Taijiquan or Qigong. He has a reputation as a real grandmaster of Taiji and Qigong and has been invited to be honorary chairman, honorary president, or advisor by more than twenty organizations worldwide.

From 1994, Master Wang Fengming lived in Finland for several years and taught Taijiquan and Qigong at the University of Helsinki and other schools. He initiated and established the European Hunyuan Taijiquan Association, and has served as its chairman to further promote Taijiquan and Qigong in Europe.

Since 1998, he has led and organized an annual European International Chen-style Hunyuan Taijiquan and Qigong Workshop in Finland, France, Germany, the Netherlands, Spain, Sweden, and the United Kingdom, which has won warm praise from enthusiasts of Taijiquan and Qigong from various countries.

In 2007, upon an invitation issued by an American university, Master Wang moved to the United States and started work there. In the same year, he also established the King of Neigong International Taiji Academy.

In 2009, Master Wang was elected as one of the Famous Taijiquan Masters in China.

In 2013, an American international school of medicine appointed him as a professor. He also received a "Successor of Chinese Non-Material Cultural Heritage" award in the same year.

Master Wang Fengming's website can be found at www.worldtaiji.com and he can be contacted via email at worldtaiji1@gmail.com.

CHAPTER I

Introduction

A. HOW TO READ THE BOOK

The Essence of Taijiquan Push-Hands and Fighting Technique derives from the techniques passed on by Grandmaster Chen Fake and his disciple, Grandmaster Feng Zhiqiang. Grandmaster Chen Fake, the ninth generation successor of Chen-style Taijiquan, is regarded as the "Taiji Number One" for his profound martial arts technique, including his legendary Taijiquan silk-reeling skill.

The cultivation approaches of the exercises of Taiji *neigong*, described in Chapter V, are a legacy of Grandmaster Hu Yaozhen, a famous exponent of Taoist Qigong. He was entitled "The Father of Modern Qigong" and "Miraculous Doctor" for his profound skills in Taoism, martial arts, and medicine.

The two grandmasters, Grandmaster Chen Fake and Grandmaster Hu Yaozhen, were distinguished modern representatives in martial arts and Qigong communities, regarded for their high standard in both morality and techniques.

Grandmaster Feng Zhiqiang is a disciple of them both. He has reached the top realm of martial arts because of his Taijiquan and Qigong, especially Taijiquan push-hands and free fighting. As the "Giant of Taiji," he is a preeminent representative of contemporary Taijiquan masters, and enjoys a high reputation at home and abroad. Based on the experience passed on from his two masters and his own practice of more than sixty years, he has innovated and developed the theory of Taiji push-hands and martial applications more practically, made their techniques more scientific, and perfected their training methods.

Push-hands training can be divided into different levels: training for beginners, training for those who want to improve their skills, training for those who want to master advanced skills, and so on. In the past, trainees were treated unequally due to the restrictions of traditional practice.

Ordinary trainees could only learn ordinary things. They could not be given the privilege and opportunities to learn more unless they became disciples.

Grandmaster Feng decided to reveal, without reservation, all the push-hands techniques once considered secret, and the present work's author carries on this open tradition. It is surely welcome news for Taijiquan enthusiasts that the traditional and private way of teaching has been substituted by an open one.

The Essence of Taijiquan Push-Hands and Fighting Technique was written to satisfy enthusiasts' desires for both health benefits and skills in martial applications, the Taijiquan *gongfu* in a real sense.

This book is composed of twelve chapters. Here, we point out the main features chapter by chapter.

In the Introduction (Chapter I), the close relationship between the exercises of Taijiquan forms and push-hands is briefly described.

In Chapter II, "Theory of Taijiquan Push-Hands and Fighting Technique," many theories are expounded, including the doctrine of yin and yang, principles of keeping balance, the theory of Taiji circling movements, and the way to determine the three lines of defense and three sections as well as the way to tackle the mistakes of *diu/pian/ding/kang* (disconnecting/leaning/directing force against force/resisting) and "double weighting" in push-hands and martial applications.

Key points concerning hands, eyes, torso, feet, and matters needing attention during push-hands and fighting are specifically passed on in Chapter III, "Main Points of Taijiquan Push-Hands and Fighting Technique."

We have selected and integrated unique and effective training methods for silk-reeling in Chapter IV, "Silk-Reeling Exercises for All Parts of the Body," tackling the problems that many new learners of Taijiquan have: stiff joints and muscles that are not relaxed. Three aspects—Points for concentration, Efficacy, and Advice—are attached to each exercise, through which we share not only the martial usage of the movements, but also the health effects of the movements.

Targeting those who have made very little progress even after having practiced for years, we emphasize the relevance of internal exercises and offer the cultivation approaches of "Exercises of Taiji Neigong" in Chapter V. The recommended way to exercise Taijiquan and internal Qigong simultaneously is summarized by Grandmaster Feng Zhiqiang and the author on the basis of experience acquired during decades of martial arts practice and teaching.

It is a shortcut for practitioners to raise the level of their internal Qigong and improve their fighting ability.

In Chapter VI, "The Thirteen Postures of Taijiquan," we present exercises on each of the eight forces of Taiji, actual application exercises for two, and combined exercises on the thirteen Taiji postures. The exercises were developed by Grandmaster Feng Zhiqiang based on his practice and research. The exercises present a revitalized approach to push-hands and martial applications.

In "Seven Training Methods for Taiji Push-Hands and Fighting Technique" (Chapter VII), we recommend seven training approaches for various styles. The approaches are suitable for practitioners at the beginning, middle, high, and advanced training stages. The practitioner may select exercises according to his level.

We introduce twenty sorts of Taiji energy to Taijiquan enthusiasts under "Essence of Taiji Energies" (Chapter VIII). They are analyzed and explained, covering the angles of energy, motion, mechanics, and human structure. The description has unity and coherence, and goes from easy to difficult. The author explores and expounds the exercises of each Taiji energy in depth in light of his experience gained in practicing Taijiquan push-hands and martial applications for many years. You may find the information original in the techniques concerning Taijiquan push-hands and martial applications.

"Seizing and Joint-Locking Techniques and Counter-Techniques" (Chapter IX) shows how to gain the initiative by performing seizing and joint-locking effectively. Also, you can learn how to gain advantage over the opponent by dispelling the opponent's joint-lock elastically and skillfully, and applying a counter-technique. Seizing and joint-locking techniques and counter-techniques vary greatly. The success of push-hands and martial applications depends largely upon the correct use of seizing and joint-locking techniques. Taking the importance of this aspect into account, we suggest that practitioners should possess some knowledge of human structure, circulation of Qi, and meridians, quite apart from the seizing and joint-locking techniques. Then practitioners will be able to seize the ligaments and joints properly, control the circulation of blood and Qi correctly, and jab at the right points with their fingers while doing seizing and joint-locking.

In Chapter X, "Leg Techniques," we present a wide variety of leg skills which are special and elastic. After reading the chapter, you will understand the meaning of "one depends 30 percent on one's fists but 70 percent on one's legs" while fighting.

The techniques of point striking are revealed in Chapter XI, "Vital Point Striking." These techniques have been hidden since ancient times. This chapter passes on the exercise methods of finger striking according to time theoretically and practically.

Some anecdotes concerning the three grandmasters are provided in Chapter XII, telling stories about Grandmaster Chen Fake, the ninth generation successor to Chen-style Taijiquan, Grandmaster Hu Yaozhen, Taoist Qigong successor, and Grandmaster Feng Zhiqiang, the "Giant of Taijiquan." Anecdotes concerning the present author, Master Wang Fengming, are also included. It is inspiring that they all demonstrated their superior martial arts skills and, at the same time, they never intimidated their opponents with their martial arts ability but won by their virtue instead.

For readability, the male pronoun is used throughout the book.

B. BASIS OF TAIJIQUAN PUSH-HANDS

Regardless of the style, size, or number of movements in its forms, all varieties of Taijiquan practiced around the world share the same content. A closer look shows that they are all based on the same philosophy, the alternation of yin and yang. They all have thirteen postures and adhere/connect/stick/follow at the core. The *National Competition Rules on Taiji Push-Hands* from the China Wushu Research Institute could be taken as a further reaffirmation that practitioners of all styles of Taijiquan push-hands share a common practice principle.

Form practice is a step to understand, utilize, and master the eight techniques and the five steps of Taiji, as well as the adhere/connect/stick/follow skills. Form practice is the method employed at the stage called "know oneself."

Taijiquan push-hands is a way to check how much and how well a practitioner has mastered the eight techniques, five steps, adhere/connect/stick/follow skills, and usage of other energies (*jin*) through form practice. It is also a tool to relearn and refine the energies and skills learned. Push-hands can be used as a way to evaluate one's level of Taijiquan.

Mechanics tells us that force starts to have effect when it is directed at an object. Force is the influence of one object on another object, or in other words, force is the influence of the applying object on the receiving object. During Taijiquan form movement practice, even though the body has forces in it, the hands or the body are not applying force to anything or receiving any outside force. During push-hands, the actual application of force is realized between the two push-hands partners. Accordingly, push-hands exercises are considered the method adopted at the stage of "knowing both oneself and the opponent."

Practice shows that push-hands can be used as the sole criterion reflecting a practitioner's level of Taijiquan, like a ruler or a mirror.

Taijiquan has gained popularity in the past hundreds of years without being assimilated by other schools of martial arts or losing its uniqueness. The cornerstones of Taijiquan are its unique theory, exercise methods, and techniques. These cornerstones will enable Taijiquan to grow even more in the future.

C. A SHORT GUIDE TO TAIJIQUAN PUSH-HANDS

Taijiquan form practice is the prerequisite for practicing Taijiquan push-hands. Good skill in push-hands is only possible through correct and skillful performance of Taijiquan forms with proper relaxation, softness, calmness, and balance. In detail, the form movements should be light, agile, and slow, the upper body and the lower body should follow each other, internal should integrate with external, and insubstantial and substantial should be clearly distinct.

Push-hands exercises can be used to further assess the correctness of form practice, usage of energies, and movements. Push-hands exercises can benefit Taijiquan form practice by teaching relaxed, soft, calm, and stable movement, by cultivating internal energy, and by developing agility. Push-hands and form movement supplement each other. You should not emphasize one at the expense of the other.

To learn the art of push-hands, we should first understand the meaning of each movement in Taijiquan. Why is a movement done the way it is? What are the relations between a movement and the structure of a human body? What are the martial applications of a movement? What is the role of internal *qi* in a movement?

Wang Zongyue said: "After you have mastered the techniques, you can gradually understand what 'understanding energy' means. After you have understood energy, you can gradually learn your opponent's intentions." The *Song of the Push-Hand* starts with the words "Be conscientious about *peng* (warding-off), *lü* (rolling-back), *ji* (pressing), and *an* (pushing). When the upper body and lower body follow each other, the opponent will find it difficult to invade." These two excerpts from the classics clearly point out the steps you should go through in practicing Taijiquan forms and push-hands as well as the level to be reached.

The word "techniques" in the first excerpt refers to the movements of each posture you make while practicing Taijiquan form movement or push-hands. "Mastering" the techniques refers to performing the movements correctly and skillfully and mastering their applications thoroughly.

The *peng* (ward-off), *lü* (roll-back), *ji* (press), and *an* (push) are called the four cardinal directions. When starting to learn push-hands, we should be clear about what *peng* is, what *lü* is, what *ji* is, and what *an* is. We should also perform them correctly and exercise them conscientiously.

After having mastered the techniques, a practitioner will be able to understand gradually how the opponent applies energy. In the Taiji terminology, this ability is called the capabilities or techniques of "listening energy" and "understanding energy."

Listening energy and understanding energy are very difficult to master. In fact, they are the subtlest techniques in push-hands. When you have learned these techniques, you should refine them continuously. Eventually you can "use a force of four ounces to deflect one thousand pounds even if the opponent attacks with enormous power" and "know the opponent, whereas the opponent does not know you," and finally reach the profound and magical boundary of "acting freely."

Listening energy and understanding energy are central to push-hands. You can rely on the two skills to conquer the opponent. Understanding energy is impossible without listening energy, so listening energy is considered the first phase in push-hands progression. Listening energy does not mean listening with the ears, but rather is a skill that relies on the control of the central nervous system and the relaxation and steadiness built into one's arms by one's normal day-to-day solo practice of Taijiquan. The arms are used to connect to the opponent and, through skin contact and interaction with the opponent, observations can be made that lead to understanding the opponent's intentions. Both training partners utilize listening energy while practicing push-hands.

Listening energy is the key skill for practicing push-hands as well as for building the ability of understanding energy. Only after knowing how to "listen" to the opponent's energy can one gradually "understand" the opponent's energy, control the opponent's energy, and further take actions according to the softness or hardness, dynamics, speed, time, position, and so on of the opponent's energy. Then one can comply with the opponent's movement, borrow the opponent's energy to neutralize or attack at the opportune moment and to the right part of the opponent's body, unbalance the opponent, and control the opponent while keeping oneself in an invincible position.

Practicing Taiji push-hands requires the practitioner to "adhere/connect/stick/follow and neither lose nor resist." "Do not lose" means that one should never separate oneself from the opponent; "do not resist" means that one should never resist the opponent's force trying to stay stationary and one should never meet the opponent's force straight against the force, that is, "head-on." It is impossible to meet these requirements without listening energy and understanding energy.

"A feather cannot be added and a fly cannot land" is how the Taijiquan classics describe listening energy. If such a level of sensitivity is put to use in push-hands, the slightest changes in the opponent's energy can be detected with great precision. This precision enables us to use just the proper amount of force in order to adhere/connect/stick/follow, "neither lose nor resist," flex or extend following the opponent, neutralize incoming energy unnoticed, and emit energy explosively.

In push-hands, without listening energy and understanding energy, one is bound to either lose contact or to resist the opponent, to react aimlessly, or to attend to one thing and neglect another. That kind of performance will not look like push-hands at all. Push-hands cannot be learnt this way, and to make things even worse, one will form bad habits which, generally speaking, will not be easy to remove. One's sensitivity may become dulled and arms rigid, making it impossible to utilize any push-hands skills.

While doing push-hands, therefore, an insubstantial and agile quality is required. Adhering to the opponent should be done in spirit, and physical contact should be light. No strength should be used for opposing the opponent, but instead the opponent's force should be followed without any unnecessary or rash actions. The energy emitted by the opponent should be judged first and then neutralized.

In push-hands, both sides are moving forward or backward, attacking or defending. They compete against each other in listening energy while dealing with each other's changes. At the same time, they compete against each other in reading signals and reacting while neither losing nor resisting.

Peng, lü, ji, and *an* may appear simple on the outside but they contain profound principles. Practitioners can improve their push-hands if they dedicate themselves to serious exploration and study for a long time. By no means can the essence of Taijiquan push-hands be learnt after simply lapping hands and making a few circles or other movements. We must start with what the Taijiquan classics emphasize: "Be conscientious about *peng, lü, ji,* and *an.* When the upper body and lower body follow each other, the opponent will find it difficult to invade."

CHAPTER II

Theory of Taijiquan Push-Hands and Fighting Technique

A. YIN AND YANG, WUJI, AND TAIJI

The theory of yin and yang is a theory for differentiating two categories of things. It illustrates the law of the unity of opposites, and that of mutual dependence and restriction. A human body is an entity in which yin and yang coexist and maintain normal biological activities and a harmonious relation with the nature outside.

The balance of yin and yang will be lost, resulting in pathological changes, if either yin or yang is waxing or waning. The balance can be adjusted and a new dynamic equilibrium regained in the continuous motion of Taijiquan, and as the equilibrium is regained, the concerned diseases will be removed and good health restored.

Wuji refers to the initial state of the space in which the sky and the earth have not yet formed by separating from each other and in which all things are yet to be created. *Wuji* means the state that was empty, chaotic, soundless, colorless, odorless, endless, and formless, and where nothing existed but all things were contained in. The intrinsic trait of *wuji* is quiescence, both internal and external.

Applying the *wuji* theory to Qigong, quiescence should be pursued first, and then, as motion is generated from extreme quiescence, yin and yang are born. Yin means stillness, and yang means motion. Quiescence is the thing-in-itself and motion is its function. Motion derives from quiescence; yang derives from yin. The inside is in motion when the outside remains still, and the inside is still when the outside is in motion. Thus, motion exists in stillness and there is stillness in motion. Motion and stillness coexist.

Intent (*yi*) and *qi* cannot flow well without *wuji* cultivation, that is, cultivation of the property "extreme stillness generates motion." "One should start with *wuji* to exercise *gong*, and then pursue conscientiously yin and yang, and opening and closing." This valuable experience handed down from generation to generation is what we should follow.

Based on the principles of yin and yang, and motion and stillness, a Chinese sage in ancient times pictured a pair of fish in an empty *wuji* circle to symbolize the two kinds of *qi*, yin and yang. The two fish were symmetric and appeared to be rotating around the circle. One of the two was black symbolizing yin and the other was white symbolizing yang. There was a white point (eye) on the black fish that symbolized that yang existed in yin— and vice versa for the white fish. The circle with the two fish illustrated the theory of mutuality between yin and yang, between motion and quiescence as well as between opening and closing. Furthermore, it illustrated that either of the two rotates around the other as the origin (while functioning as the other's origin) and that the two compensate each other and that all things are created by the two. It is the symbol of Taiji we have today. Taijiquan was named Taiji because it absorbed the dialectical philosophy of yin and yang, *wuji*, and *taiji*.

Distinguishing features of Taijiquan

- *The coexistence of motion and stillness*: *Wuji* is stillness or quiescence. Motion is generated from extreme stillness, from which *taiji* derives. Yin and yang separate from each other when *taiji* is in motion. Taijiquan is a practice to pursue motion while in stillness, to pursue stillness while in motion, and to pursue the coexistence of motion and stillness. Practitioners may pursue motion in stillness of *wuji*, pursue stillness in motion while doing Taijiquan forms, pursue good health by nourishing *qi*, or pit stillness against motion in push-hands. However, no matter what they seek, they cannot do without the word pair "motion and stillness." Motion and stillness exist in the entire Taijiquan practice.

- *The opposition and unity*: Every movement of Taijiquan has changes between opening and closing, insubstantial and substantial, motion and stillness, and softness and hardness, which indicates that the pairs of opposites are also united. One divides into two that are yin and yang; two combine into one that is *taiji*. They interconnect, interdepend, and interact, which ensures that the whole body moves in unison.

  For example, up and down, left and right, front and back, internal and external, forward and backward, upward and downward, bend and extend, clockwise and counterclockwise, and store and emit are pairs where one part cannot exist without the other. Accordingly, the rules of symmetry and balance are emphasized in Taijiquan theory as follows: "There must be a movement going backward if there is a movement going forward; there must be a movement going downward if there is a movement going upward; there must be a movement going to the left if there is one going to the right; and there must be a movement going inward if there is a movement going outward."

- *Inter-transformation*: Yin and yang are two sides of a contradiction. They coexist, affect each other, permeate each other, adjust each other, assist and use each other, and take the other side as their own origin. The relationships between them are well shown in Taijiquan; for example: "Move downward before moving upward; move rightward before moving leftward; move backward before moving forward; close before opening; open before closing; transform hardness into softness; and accumulate softness making hardness."

  The process of transforming one thing into another is a process in which the thing first changes quantitatively and then qualitatively. The practice of Taijiquan is in line with the same principle. Taijiquan is also considered motion of mind/intent and *qi*. The following effects of Qigong exercise can be obtained provided a practitioner concentrates on the *dantian* while performing Taijiquan: extreme stillness generating motion, extreme motion generating stillness, refining (cultivating) essence (*jing*) into *qi*, refining *qi* into spirit (*shen*), refining spirit into void, *qi* arriving when mind/intent arrives, and power arriving when *qi* arrives.

  Without exception, a push-hands practitioner progresses from the primary stage of "visible energy" to the middle stage named "invisible energy," and then to the high stage entitled "neutralizing energy" (*hua jin*). The process of improvement, or the cultivation of one's *gongfu*, is also a transforming process from quantitative changes to qualitative changes, and the transforming process is actually constant improvement.

In short, with Taijiquan having the above-mentioned features, the process of exercising push-hands is a process of adjusting yin and yang, motion and stillness, emptiness and solidness, hardness and softness, and quickness and slowness in order to balance them. The adjusting and transforming activities exist in the entire process.

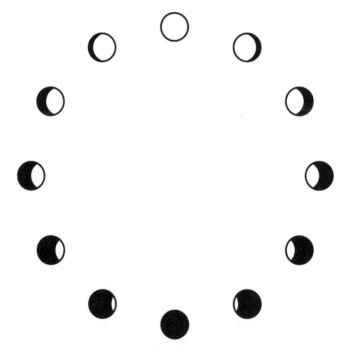

FIGURE 2.1 TRANSFORMATION OF YIN AND YANG

B. PRINCIPLES OF KEEPING BALANCE

Maintaining balance can be done by adjusting parts of the body. Even when balance falls out of the scope of centered and upright (*zhong zheng*), adjustments in body, footwork, and/or hand techniques may be used to regain balance and get back to the centered and upright scope.

The following are the commonly used ways of maintaining balance in Taiji push-hands:

1. *Stable balance*: A type of balance that is best described by a circular cone put upright like a pagoda. Its base lies flat on the ground and

the tip points upward. In this position, the cone is most stable. It is considered to be in a state of stable balance as its center of gravity is low and centered and its upper part is much lighter than its lower part.

In Taijiquan push-hands, stable balance refers to a state where the torso is kept upright and in the center without tilting, where the upper body and the lower body follow each other, and where all parts of the body move in unison. The state is kept regardless of the direction of the movement when moving and regardless of the assumed posture when not moving.

FIGURE 2.2 STABLE BALANCE

2. *Unstable balance*: A type of balance that is best described by a circular cone put upside down, which means that the tip is on the ground and the round base is at the top, like a standing awl. In this position, the circular cone, with a heavy head and light feet, is in a very vulnerable and temporary balance. Therefore, it is said to have unstable balance.

In Taijiquan push-hands, a state of unstable balance is caused by leaning or bending in some direction or having the center of gravity otherwise out of control. In such a situation, making a big step, jumping up, or spinning around can be attempted to get back in balance at the time the feet land on the ground. A Taijiquan proverb says: "There is attack and defense in keeping balance. Keep balance actively, and you can take the initiative any time; try to keep balance passively, and you will land yourself in a passive position all the time."

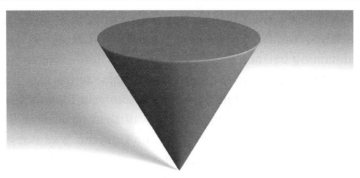

FIGURE 2.3 UNSTABLE BALANCE

3. *Supported balance.* Temporary balance can be obtained by forming a jointed chassis which is like a one-way supported or mutually supported body. As an example, when standing on a bus and the driver brakes suddenly, a passenger without a support leans, bends, or may even fall down because of the force of inertia. The passenger will regain balance if he manages to hold something with the hand for support or lean against something. This example shows how the principle of supported balance functions in our daily life. In Taijiquan push-hands and fighting technique, the principle can be used as a basis for developing techniques to regain balance.

   For example, in push-hands, when the opponent uses *lü* (rolling back) and leads your center of gravity out of the centered and upright scope, forcing you to lean forward in a sudden movement, you can, from this extremely unbalanced state, use footwork to move rapidly forward, lean on the opponent's body with the torso or the limbs to gain a temporary balance, and then use *ji* (pressing) to attack back. In this way, you can not only adjust and restore your balance but also attack the opponent. This example shows a practical application of the principle of supported balance in Taijiquan push-hands or fighting.

   The method of supported balance should be used properly. When trying to get supported by the opponent, you should take precautions against the possibility that the opponent may be using empty energy and, instead of getting supported, you end up falling as if a pair of crutches were suddenly removed.

4. *Collision balance.* Balance of an object is restored by the counteracting force when a collision happens between the object and another object.

In Taijiquan push-hands and martial applications, some techniques are based on the principle of collision balance for regaining or maintaining balance.

For example, when the opponent uses *cai* (plucking) energy to guide you into emptiness, you can adjust your footwork and follow the opponent's energy in a timely way, then push or collide against the opponent and restore your balance. In this way, not only is the danger changed into safety, but you can also attack actively. This example represents a practical application of the principle of collision balance in Taijiquan push-hands or fighting.

5. *Adaptive balance*: When a spheroid or a wooden bar placed horizontally is rolling, its center of gravity will never be beyond the scope of safety. This kind of balance is called adaptive balance, which means that an object is in balance wherever it is.

    Mechanics tells us that round objects are the most capable of bearing outside forces and encounter the least resistance. Rotating movements can be used to change the angles or directions of the forces emitted by the opponent or those emitted by the practitioner. Also, rotation can be used to change the speed of movements.

    For forms or push-hands practice, it is emphasized that all movements should be circular without being convex or concave, having sharp corners, or having any other imperfections. A practitioner's torso and four limbs should be bow-shaped and he should be able to handle all directions and master the application of silk-reeling. All of the aforementioned represent practical applications of the law of circular movement in Taijiquan.

    For example, when a pushing force is applied to you, you should rotate from the waist to the left or right for neutralizing. When falling down to the ground, you should bring your limbs closer to the body and roll for self-protection and balance-restoring adjustment.

    The application of silk-reeling to Taiji push-hands is also an application of the principle of adaptive balance or "adapting to any circumstance" to push-hands. Although the spiral movements of the entire body and the corresponding insubstantial/substantial changes on the feet are somewhat different from the principle of adaptive balance, they do result in similar effects.

FIGURE 2.4 ADAPTIVE BALANCE

To maintain the body in balance, a practitioner should have the necessary capability for symmetric adjustment; otherwise the efforts to maintain balance are a mere formality. The law on symmetric adjustment in Taijiquan push-hands can be summarized as follows:

1. If you intend to move upward, you must first move downward.

2. If you intend to move to the left, you must first go to the right.

3. When moving forward, there must be a movement backward for support.

4. Keep attracting and tying together the upper and lower, and the left and right.

5. Stretch and elongate, and look for the straight in the curved.

These five rules on symmetric adjustment for balance can be applied to Taiji push-hands. However, the specific skills are too detailed and complicated to explore and master without demonstration and guidance from an experienced teacher. Nevertheless, it is the complication and difficulties that make the theory and skills so fascinating.

C. TURN AT A TOUCH WITH THE LOWER BACK AS AXIS

In Taijiquan theory, "turn at a touch with the lower back as axis" is emphasized as there are many other axes in the human body. In fact, each part of the body can make local rotations. Silk-reeling is used to adjust all the rotations between the various parts and various joints. There are four main axes concerning the rotation of the whole body:

1. *Vertical axis*: Runs from the head to the feet through the whole body. This axis is what "the upper body aligns with the lower body" (central and upright line) of Taijiquan theory emphasizes.

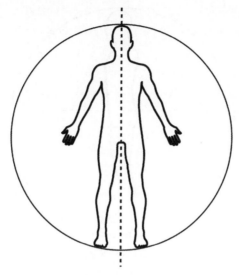

FIGURE 2.5 VERTICAL AXIS

2. *Transverse axis*: Runs horizontally through the two sides of the body. A forward roll around this axis is done when leaning forward, and a backward roll around this axis is done when leaning backward.

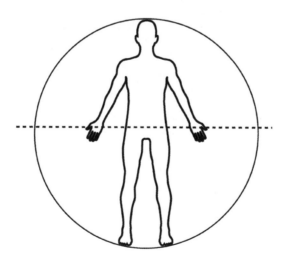

FIGURE 2.6 TRANSVERSE AXIS

3. *Anteroposterior axis:* Runs horizontally through the front and back of the body. Rotation around this axis is done when shifting to the left or to the right.

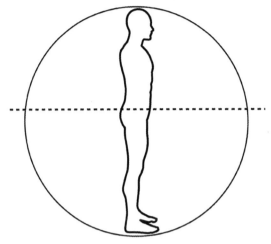

FIGURE 2.7 ANTEROPOSTERIOR AXIS

4. *Sub-axes:* Sub-axes are local axes running through various parts or joints in the human body, including the neck, back, waist, shoulders, elbows, wrists, hips, knees, and feet. Sub-axes are widely used in push-hands and martial applications.

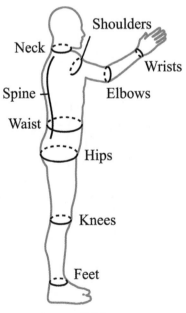

FIGURE 2.8 SUB-AXES

First of all, we need to understand the basic principle of movements concerning the axes. An axis is a formless line which goes through a rotating object. Sometimes it is a visible axis like the ones mounted in a generator, a car, or an airplane, and sometimes an invisible axis like the ones that "exist" in a human body, a ball-shaped object, or a planet. As long as an object rotates or spins, there must be an axis or axle mounted somewhere. In our context, an axis can be taken as an invisible line running through the center of a spinning or rotating object.

A spinning object, be it on the ground or in the sky, must have at least one axis around which it spins. Otherwise there would be no rotation. When in rotation, the object and the axis which it is revolving around are at a right angle.

In Taijiquan push-hands or fighting techniques, when a practitioner stands on the ground rotating in the horizontal plane, the axis runs through the center of gravity and the pivot point. In this case, the axis is named the "central axis," "vertical axis," or "upright axis." The central axis running from the head to the feet is the axis repeatedly emphasized by the Taiji theory, that is, "use the lower back as the axis." Also, it is the axis used most frequently in Taijiquan push-hands or fighting.

Provided that the lower back is kept upright, the central axis will be upright and straight. Revolving around an upright axis, the practitioner will be stable and powerful, regardless of the direction or the range of the revolution.

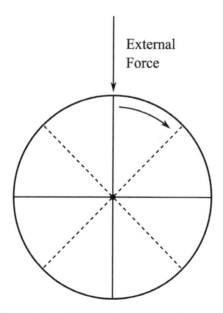

External
Force

FIGURE 2.9 TURN AT A TOUCH WITH THE LOWER BACK AS AXIS

Just as with a door axis, where the balance of the door depends on whether the axis is upright, it goes without saying that if the central axis is neither upright nor straight, the balance of the center of gravity will be affected. A crooked torso indicates that the central axis is neither upright nor straight. Consequently, the position will be unstable and unbalanced. How could push-hands or fighting techniques be performed well from an unstable position? That is why this technique is so strongly emphasized.

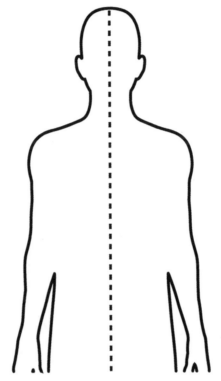

FIGURE 2.10 CENTRAL AND UPRIGHT LINE OR CENTRAL AXIS

D. THE THREE LINES OF DEFENSE AND THE THREE SEGMENTS

When attacking and defending in Taijiquan push-hands and fighting, utilize the "three lines of defense" as follows (see Figure 2.11):

- The first line of defense: hands and feet.

- The second line of defense: elbows and knees.

- The third line of defense: shoulders and hips.

The theory of Taijiquan states: "Use fists when the opponent is at a distance, elbow when at short range, and lean when pressing close." The distance in attacking and defending is divided into these three lines of defense.

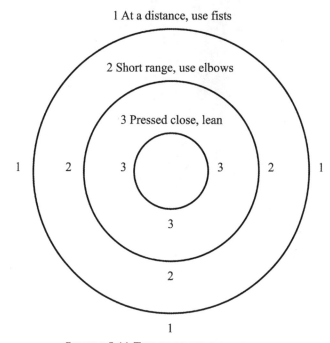

FIGURE 2.11 THREE LINES OF DEFENSE

In Taiji push-hands and fighting technique, the body is divided into three segments as follows (see Figure 2.12):

- Upper segment: above the level of the shoulder–collar bone joints.

- Middle segment: between the level of the shoulder–collar bone joints and the navel level.

- Lower segment: below the navel level.

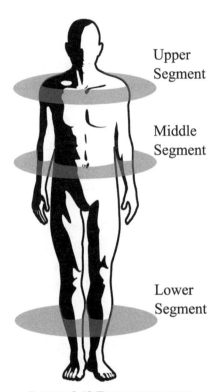

Upper Segment

Middle Segment

Lower Segment

FIGURE 2.12 THREE SEGMENTS

The theory of Taijiquan push-hands and fighting advises practitioners to "focus on hand techniques in the upper segment, focus on body techniques in the middle segment, and focus on foot techniques in the lower segment," and it also tells us that "Taiji is on the head, the five elements in the body, and the eight diagrams beneath the feet."

E. OCCUPY THE FRONT GATE OR
SNATCH THE SIDE GATE

During Taijiquan push-hands or fighting practice, the practitioners either take the initiative to attack or defend and counter-attack. In any case, they cannot do so without the two methods of occupying the front (or central) gate and snatching the side gate.

The front gate means the position where the centered and upright line lies. Occupying the opponent's front gate gives a practitioner an advantageous position. When attacking from such a position, the distance is too short for the opponent to judge and react properly. The practitioner can cover the short distance and hit the opponent within an extremely short time in order to beat the opponent or create favorable conditions to do so.

Most of the vital parts in a human body are on the centerline. A frontal attack may enable a practitioner to hit the opponent more effectively and destroy the opponent's fighting ability more easily.

Take defense followed by a counter-attack as an example. When the opponent initiates a frontal attack at you, regardless of the angle of the attack, he must leave some of his weak points exposed. Utilizing the fact, you can redirect and neutralize the attack while launching a frontal attack at his weak points. It is very difficult for the opponent to avoid your attack because the distance is so short. The Taijiquan classics express this situation as: "When the opponent does not move, I do not move; when the opponent is about to move, I move first."

When the opponent attacks with fists, his center of gravity must be on one side. If he uses his right fist, his weight will be on the right side, whereas the left side will be insubstantial. You should neutralize his right-side attack and make a counter-attack upon his left side. If he attacks with his left fist, his center of gravity will be on the left side and the right side will be weak. In this case, you should neutralize his left fist and counter-attack his right side.

As described above, staying clear of the opponent's main force and striking promptly at his weak points enables one to get twice the result with half the effort. The above also shows the importance of protecting one's own centered and upright state while aiming to destroy that of the opponent.

Treading into the front gate is one of the most effective ways for occupying the front gate. As told by a proverb: "Three tenths relies on the fists and seven tenths relies on the legs." Treading into the front gate, generally speaking, means occupying an advantageous position using footwork to destroy the opponent's centered and upright state and to break his balance. When attacking, the effective result can be that the opponent's root is cut, which will not only greatly weaken the opponent's ability to defend or counter-attack, but also put him in a passive position and make it practically impossible for him to defend effectively.

The so-called side gate means both sides of the opponent's arms and legs which function for self-protection. Snatching the side gate, or "taking the side," means to change a passive situation into an active one through attacking the side gate when the opponent is in a better situation, well prepared, or his central gate is already well protected.

For example, when the opponent attacks with a fist, you can first redirect and neutralize his force, and then step forward sideways in order to get to his side. At this point, attacking his weak points will bring a certain victory.

One of the purposes of snatching the side gate is to avoid engaging in frontal battle with the opponent. This is good not only for self-protection and attacking the opponent, but also for making the opponent's force enter into emptiness, rendering his attack ineffective, and putting the opponent into a passive situation. The rules of Taijiquan dictate us to "guide the opponent to enter into emptiness; give up oneself and follow the opponent; make yin and yang change into each other." Following these rules makes it easy to attack the opponent and, conversely, difficult for the opponent to attack.

Also in Baguazhang (eight-diagram palm), great importance is attached to "staying clear from the front (frontal attack) and hitting from the side." While attacking or defending, instead of engaging squarely from the front, a Baguazhang practitioner will utilize body techniques and other skills to occupy the side gate, and then take the advantage to attack.

Another purpose of snatching the side gate is to "give up yourself and follow the opponent" and "guide the opponent to enter into emptiness." In other words, the purpose is to use the opponent's negligence to your benefit.

When the side gate is successfully occupied, the opponent's vulnerable side and back will be exposed. From this position, a blow will land on the target as long as it is struck—one of the advantages of borrowing force and emitting force, and taking the side gate.

During a fight, treading into the central gate or taking the side gate should be used according to the situation. A proverb says: "Step straight ahead if the situation is favorable to you, or if it is not, step on either side instead."

In general, if the opponent is physically weak, his *gongfu* is not high level, or he is in an otherwise worse situation than you, adopt the tactic of occupying the central gate, as in the proverb, "Tread forward and make your way between the opponent's feet; upper and lower body go forward together to destroy any resistance." However, if the opponent is strong, his *gongfu* is higher than yours, and his fighting technique is superior, you should utilize the tactic of snatching the side gate. Keep away from the opponent's main force, occupy a proper side position, and attack. Pit the weak against the strong and gain victory.

F. HOW TO TACKLE THE PROBLEMS OF DIU, PIAN, AND DING/KANG

1. How to tackle the problem of "disconnecting" (diu)

First of all let us discuss how "disconnection," or *diu*, happens in push-hands. Disconnection means separating from the opponent because of a failure to stick to the opponent's limbs or torso or because of a failure to follow the changes in the opponent's energy during push-hands. For example, if you do not move forward or just stay where you are, or even drag backward, when your opponent is leading you with *lü* (rolling-back) energy, you will disconnect from the opponent.

The physical disconnection of the limbs or the trunk is called "losing touch," whereas a failure in following the opponent's energy is called "losing energy." Losing touch is one of the situations of losing energy. Losing energy goes against the fundamental principles of push-hands: it indicates that the practitioner fails in using the "adhere/connect/stick/follow" techniques.

How to correct the mistake of losing energy then? The right way is sticking to the principle of following the opponent's energy and movement while being led. For example, you should move one foot and two inches or even a little longer forward following the opponent's energy if he applies *lü* energy and leads you a distance of one foot. You can then break his route of energy, be ahead of him everywhere, and put yourself in an active position instead of a passive one while putting the opponent in a passive position.

It is a relevant case of losing energy when the practitioner does not employ the basic adhere/connect/stick/follow push-hands skills correctly. The adhere/connect/stick/follow skills are effective in overcoming losing energy.

After long-term practice, a practitioner can learn all the changes in the opponent's intent, directions, and routes of energy by relying on skin contact and sensing changes in movements. He can sense whether the energy or movements are going forward or backward, leftward or rightward, and upward or downward, and whether the energy is substantial or insubstantial, questioning or emitting, and so on.

The adhering and sticking skills are fundamental in push-hands. "Listening energy" (*ting jin*) cannot be understood without understanding them. However, adhering and sticking to your opponent too tightly may restrict your ability to listen, slow down your ability to react, and even cause rigidity and stagnation which result in *ding* (directing your force against the opponent's force). On the other hand, adhering and sticking to the opponent too loosely may cause losing energy.

How can we correct the above mistakes and adhere and stick to a proper extent? It requires us to follow the opponent's movements and energy— do not move when the opponent does not move, and move first when the opponent is about to move. We should slowly accumulate experience in our long-term practice.

When practicing the adhere and stick skills, you should adhere to the opponent without any separation no matter how the opponent moves or changes his energy paths. With proper application of adhere and stick, the opponent has no way to apply any of his skills or energy, whereas you can detect changes in the opponent's energy path, his weak points, the target of his force, and his center of gravity. Then you can continue by neutralizing the opponent's force, leading and moving the opponent's center of gravity, and finally attacking. This process is commonly stated as "use stillness to overcome movement and then attack."

When practicing the connect and follow skills, do not stick to any fixed postures. When the opponent makes big movements, make big movements; when he makes small movements, make small movements as well.

In short, you should adhere/connect/stick/follow and keep following the changes made by the opponent closely, no matter how he changes. To be able to employ adhere/connect/stick/follow correctly to change one's own energy paths and usage is considered understanding energy.

However, any meaningless or aimless movements in push-hands should be avoided. When the opponent's limbs or trunk do not move, some practitioners tend to move just to use the adhere/connect/stick/follow skills. Initiating movements without the intent of attacking or defending are opportunities that the opponent can exploit.

2. How to tackle the problem of "tilting" (pian)

Failing to maintain the centered and upright state and leaning to some direction is called "tilting," or *pian*. Tilting is also one of the main mistakes in Taijiquan push-hands. This mistake is caused by a failure to relax part or the whole of the body or a failure to sink *qi* to the *dantian* while trying to bear an incoming force. Failing to neutralize an incoming force, in order to stay centered and upright, when a rigid force is not enough for coping with the incoming force, is also a possible cause.

How to correct the mistake of tilting then? In push-hands, it is required to align the upper body with the lower, to relax the whole body, and to sink *qi* to the *dantian*. Whether the body is centered and upright and whether the upper body aligns with the lower can be taken as yardsticks to check whether these requirements have been met. If the requirements indeed have been met, the centered and upright state can be kept in push-hands and the body will be round, agile, light, relaxed, and calm.

Bowing, tilting back or shaking the head, tilting to the left or right, or being absent-minded are mistakes that need to be urgently addressed in push-hands. As summarized by a proverb: "With head bowed and body bent, skills cannot be good." When practicing push-hands, the body should always be centered and upright and the upper body and the lower body should always be coordinated.

To relax the body and sink *qi* to the *dantian*, all the organs, muscles, and joints all over the body should be relaxed. Then, to get rid of rigidity and disharmony in the body, first the "three external harmonies" should be reached, then gradually the "three internal harmonies," and finally "the integration of the internal and the external."

The three internal harmonies are: (1) the heart/mind (*xin*) harmonizes with the intent, (2) the intent (*yi*) harmonizes with *qi*, and (3) *qi* harmonizes with physical power. The three external harmonies are: (1) the hands harmonize with the feet, (2) the elbows harmonize with the knees, and (3) the shoulders harmonize with the hips. The three internal harmonies and three external harmonies are developed with long-term practice of forms and Qigong. In summary, the internal integrates with the external; when one part moves, all parts move; when one part closes, all parts close; and all are applicable to the five inner organs and all parts of the body.

In push-hands, relaxation and the harmonies should be dealt with dialectically. Each of them should be done within a proper range. Relaxation should be distinguished from slackness or weakness. Relaxation makes the joints agile and *qi* sink to the *dantian*. After energy is harmonized through relaxation, the capability to neutralize and emit energy in any circumstance will be improved. When facing a big and well-trained opponent, a practitioner is apt to get nervous, which will make his body rigid, muscles tense, and movements slow and stiff. When the practitioner in this kind of state tries to receive an incoming force, he will easily make the mistakes of tilting and/or resisting. However, relaxing too much, up to a point of turning slack, is also not correct. You should go by the rule "no excess, no deficiency."

3. How to tackle the problems of "directing force against force/resisting" (ding/kang)

In push-hands competitions, using adhere/connect/stick/follow, "guide the opponent to enter into emptiness," and "use four ounces to defeat one thousand pounds" among others is considered to be in accordance with Taiji's principles. Using rigid force, directing force against the opponent's force, or stubbornly resisting the opponent's force is not considered to be in accordance with Taiji's principles, and such mistakes are called *ding/kang*.

Ding/kang can be caused by inadequate spiraling and neutralization; faulty, non-round, non-integrated energy; slow and/or inadequate change of energy; poor listening energy; and/or double-heaviness. For the most part, *ding/kang* happens when one has superior strength compared to the opponent and one has the chance to beat the opponent simply by strength, but in doing so, one is neglecting to use any skills and will automatically make the mistake of *ding/kang*.

Ding is a force directed at an angle of 180 degrees towards the opponent's force, whereas attempting to win by brute force is *kang*. *Kang* is also the usual reason for the "fighting bulls" phenomenon in push-hands.

How to correct the mistakes of *ding/kang* then? More attention should be paid to practicing spiraling and neutralization to pursue roundness and integration of energy. Also, the capability for reacting to changes in situation should be developed through improving the sensibility of listening energy.

Top priority should be given to developing listening energy. Through listening energy one can learn to know the opponent's energy thoroughly and one can eventually reach the state of "the opponent does not know me, while I know the opponent." After reaching that state, one can utilize one's own insubstantial point to search the substantial point in the opponent's body.

Compared to listening and watching, the tactile sensation of the skin is much more important for probing the directions and dynamics of the incoming energy. This listening energy is an internal energy gradually developed mainly through push-hands exercises. It is light, agile, heavy, elaborate, and tenacious.

The better one's *gongfu* is, the more sensitive one's tactile sensation is. The skin and hairs of the entire body exhale and inhale as well as open and close; a magnetic field is induced inside the body, which makes the tactile sensation extremely sensitive.

After a sensitive listening energy has been developed, a conditional reflex will be formed in the cerebral cortex which enables a practitioner to neutralize incoming energy whenever necessary. At this stage, the practitioner can understand the state of "a feather cannot be added without getting stuck." The listening energy exercises are steps on the ladder of *gongfu*. As in the proverb "perseverance spells success," only unremitting efforts will help you to develop listening energy ability and use it well.

Another effective approach for eliminating the mistakes of *ding/kang* in push-hands is silk-reeling. This is composed of various circular movements driven by the spiraling internal energy.

The silk-reeling exercises can be divided into inward spiral, outward spiral, large spiral, small spiral, left spiral, right spiral, front spiral, back spiral, upright spiral, oblique spiral, and others. However, there are just two general categories: the *shun* ("going with") spiral and the *ni* ("going against") spiral.

Assuming an initial position of holding a hand so that the palm faces downward, an example of the *shun* spiral would be turning the hand so that the little finger moves downward and the thumb moves upward. From the same initial position, turning the hand so that the little finger moves upward and the thumb moves downward would produce the *ni* spiral. Moving an elbow outward, as in opening, is a *ni* spiral, whereas moving an elbow inward, as in closing, is a *shun* spiral.

In push-hands, spiral movements, along with extension and contraction, should be used to produce circular movements. Circular movements can redirect an incoming force as well as one's own force and change the speeds of movements. Furthermore, rotation generates dynamic force.

The silk-reeling exercises help in reaching a state in which "when one part moves, all parts move" inside and outside the entire body. In addition, all the systems of nerves, breath, circulation, meridians and collaterals, muscles, and the five inner organs as well as all other parts of the body get exercised simultaneously. Internally, persistent silk-reeling practice gives exercise to essence (*jing*), *qi*, and spirit (*shen*), and externally, it exercises ligaments, bones, and skin. The practice makes *qi* run through the meridians and collaterals and get into the bone marrow, and ultimately cultivate the *hunyuan qi*.

Applied in push-hands, silk-reeling appears as circular movements, making all rotary parts or joints of the body move spirally, including the so-called "eighteen balls" of the body: the neck, chest, waist, abdomen, buttocks, shoulders, elbows, wrists, hips, knees, and feet. Silk-reeling allows the eighteen balls to be merged into one big Taiji ball. Furthermore, silk-reeling enables one to lead spirally and advance spirally. It makes every movement a Taiji movement.

A good silk-reeling skill will allow you to move freely according to your will in push-hands. The opponent will feel as if in a whirlpool, while you will seem to be like a roly-poly toy, constantly in an invincible position.

Bearing in mind the qualities of silk-reeling mentioned above, it should be clear that applying silk-reeling in push-hands is an effective way to eliminate the *ding/kang* mistakes. Practice the silk-reeling skills seriously in order to further improve your push-hands standard.

G. HOW TO CORRECT THE MISTAKE OF "DOUBLE-HEAVINESS"

"Double-heaviness" is a term in Taijiquan used to describe the phenomenon of "equal weight." In push-hands, a failure to do timely adjustments in hand techniques, body techniques, footwork, yin/yang, insubstantial/substantial, and/or hardness/softness may result in equal weight.

Analysis of the occurrence of double-heaviness in push-hands reveals that double-heaviness exists in the following situations:

1. Hands are double-heavy.

2. Torso is double-heavy.

3. Feet are double-heavy.

4. Two forces (of both sides) resist each other.

5. Two forces (of both sides) contend against each other.

An inevitable consequence of double-heaviness is that "a large amount of power defeats a small amount, and strong defeat weak," which is against the Taijiquan rules that advise to "give up oneself and follow the opponent, guide the opponent to enter into emptiness, borrow and use energy for defeating a large amount of power with a small amount, beat the strong with the weak, and use skills to defeat an opponent." Besides, double-heaviness cannot embody the distinguishing features of Taijiquan push-hands and fighting art, and with double-heaviness, Taijiquan push-hands and fighting art would not be any different from other martial arts.

"Heaviness on one side enables one to yield and follow; double-heaviness makes one stagnant," as mentioned in the Taiji classics, means that when the opponent emits energy, you should adjust yin and yang, substantial and insubstantial, and hardness and softness accordingly. You should load your energy on one side and move to the left or right, up or down, or forward or backward, to avoid resisting the opponent's substantial energy while keeping your energy paths unimpeded. Double-heaviness will be produced and energy paths will stagnate if you use heavy force to resist the energy released by the opponent.

In the sentence "double-heaviness makes one stagnant," "stagnant" means sluggish and being hindered, and in push-hands its manifestation is when the energy paths of both sides are blocked. Flowing water is often used as a metaphor for energy, especially incoming (the opponent's) energy. If you divert rushing water (incoming energy) to pass by your side, the rapids will not lash you. At the same time, if you apply the principle of inertia and take the opportunity to borrow energy and emit it in the direction you lead, it will certainly force the opponent's center of gravity to move beyond the scope of centered and upright and make him lose balance or fall. The principles of mechanics tell us that for every force acting on an object, the object must be made to bear the force in order for the force to move the object; if the object is not made to bear the force, the force is an example of "useless energy."

In Taiji push-hands, two forces directed at each other or resisting each other is called double-heaviness. Another form of double-heaviness is pulling or dragging against the opponent's force. The resulting situation is "two forces pulling each other." The former and the latter type of double-heaviness are essentially the same—only the directions of the forces are the opposite. Therefore, two forces pulling each other is also categorized as double-heaviness.

The "pulling or dragging" in the above means trying to pull or drag the opponent when the opponent does not move at all or when the opponent even struggles in the opposite direction. In such a situation, a stalemate might ensue, just like when playing tug of war, and if either side loosens the grip, the other will fall backward.

It is advisable for you to take advantage of the above mistakes in push-hands. When the opponent pulls or drags, instead of struggling to the opposite direction, you might as well follow and add your force to the opponent. Thus, you can make the opponent fall easily. When doing Taiji push-hands, one must comply with the rules of "following the opponent's direction, borrowing force from the opponent, and then releasing energy; giving up oneself and following the opponent; and guiding the opponent to enter into emptiness." If you can adjust yin and yang, substantial and insubstantial, and hardness and softness in a timely way, and "guide the opponent's power into emptiness and immediately attack," you will be able to "get the desired effect and use skill to defeat your opponent."

CHAPTER III

Main Points of Taijiquan Push-Hands and Fighting Technique

A. BODY TECHNIQUES

1. Stand with the body centered and upright, without tilting

The law of Taiji is the law of the mean. It postulates no tilting or leaning, and no excess or deficiency. Taijiquan may be a small *Tao*, but it stems from the true *Tao* of Taiji.

Regardless of whether the internal or external, spirit or outward appearance, or motions or their martial applications are concerned, the golden mean should be taken whenever adjusting the aspects of yin and yang, opening and closing, withdrawing and releasing, substantial and insubstantial, and motion and stillness. In short, the golden mean should be kept in everything. The *qi* of the Middle Jiao can then pass through the entire body.

When standing with the body centered and upright without tilting or leaning, there is no need to worry about falling when being pushed. When there is no excess or deficiency, there will be no mistakes of *ding* (fighting force head-on), *bian* (having too weak a contact), *diu* (disconnecting) or *kang* (resisting). A practitioner who has abundant *qi* of the Middle Jiao can comply perfectly with attacks.

"Centered and upright" means no tilting or leaning and no excess or deficiency. In push-hands, centered and upright is reflected in the body techniques as a requirement to stand with the body centered and upright and to neither tilt nor lean. From the top of the head to the heels, the upper body aligns with the lower body, and the entire body is internally and externally well balanced in all directions.

Concerning the requirements of centered and upright, priority is given to the centered and upright trunk, whereas centered and upright limbs are supplementary, although they influence the state of the body. Of course, a perfect centered and upright state depends on all parts of the whole body.

The human body can be divided into three sections. The tip section refers to the arms, the middle section to the torso, and the root (base) section to the legs. Also, there are five bows in the body. Each arm is a bow, each leg is a bow, and the torso is a bow. A practitioner can maintain force in all directions and keep the entire body centered and upright without tilting if he, supported by the internal *qi*, can link the three sections into one and form the five bows and unite them into one.

The first point

The neck is erect and the head is upright, led upward by an insubstantial energy.

The head is where the six yang meridians converge, and it is considered the master of the entire body. An upright head fixes the body to a naturally centered and upright posture. An erect neck makes the two muscles behind the neck erect. The two muscles are considered the channels for the *qi* of the Middle Jiao to flow up and down. "An insubstantial energy leading the head up" enables spirit to rise, *qi* of the Middle Jiao to run through all over the body, and spirit to pass through to the head.

"An insubstantial energy leading the head up" really means that the leading up is insubstantial, that is, only a matter of intent, nothing more. Neither excess nor deficiency is correct. *Qi* will be detained in the brain if the head is "led upward" too much, whereas *qi* will be detained in the chest if the head is not led upward enough. Diseases will be caused either way.

The second point

The chest is insubstantial and the abdomen substantial; the upper body is insubstantial and the lower substantial.

The mind should be insubstantial and calm, and the chest should be relaxed and empty. An insubstantial mind makes the chest empty; an empty chest makes the diaphragm sink, both sides of the chest descend, and the abdomen substantial in a natural way. *Qi* descending to the *dantian* makes the upper body insubstantial and the lower substantial, the upper agile and twistable, and the lower strong like a huge rock. Calm mind and tranquil *qi* make turbid *qi* descend and clear *qi* ascend, which makes separation of yin and yang clear.

The third point

> The waist is collapsed, the buttocks are tucked in, and the spine is straight and upright.

The waist is a pivot between the upper body and the lower body. The waist should be soft and insubstantial, as softness and insubstantiality enable it to sink down. In addition, the buttocks should be tucked in to make the waist sink down. The *huiyin* acupoint needs to be pulled up, as *qi* will not leak out from *huiyin* when it is pulled up. When the waist is flat and the buttocks are tucked in, the energy of the waist will be able to penetrate down, the upper body will be insubstantial, the middle body will be agile, the lower body will be heavy and steady, and all the power in the entire body can be integrated at the *dantian*.

When the buttocks are tucked in, the sacrum will be powerful, the *weilü* acupoint will be centered and vertical, and, with the head being led upward by an insubstantial energy, the spine will be upright. The area of *mingmen* will then open naturally and the *qi* of the Middle Jiao will be able to pass through the spine like a thread from *baihui* to *huiyin*, and the body bow will be formed.

The fourth point

> The shoulders are relaxed and sunk, and the elbows point downward.

The agility of the arms depends on the shoulders. The shoulders are the pivots of the arms. If the shoulders are not relaxed, rotation of the arms will not be agile. The shoulders should be relaxed and sunk, and after persistent and devoted practice, the shoulder joints will have wider clearances and the arms seem to hang on the shoulders. When the *qi* of the Middle Jiao flows into the clearances at the shoulder joints, the shoulders will be able to sink, and when the *qi* of the Middle Jiao flows from the clearances at the shoulder joints to the arms, the arms will be calm, insubstantial, and agile.

The elbows should point down, or otherwise the shoulders will not be sunk, *qi* will float up, the energy in the body will not integrate, and the centered and upright state of the body will be affected. Sinking the elbows contributes to sinking the shoulders. Sinking the elbows and the shoulders contributes to linking together the three sections of the arms, namely the shoulders, elbows, and hands, including the fingertips. When the three sections of the arms can be linked together, the arm bows will be formed.

In other words, "the shoulders should be sunk, and the elbows should point downward." It does not matter how the hands and arms rotate. Movement can be upward or downward, or leftward or rightward.

The fifth point

> The hips should be in a seated posture and the knees should be bent and vertically aligned with the hips.

The hips are the pivots of the legs, but the relevance of the hips is much more than that. Whether the energy of the waist can go downward, whether the entire body can be in harmony, whether the upper body and the lower body can follow each other, whether the qi of the Middle Jiao can pass through everywhere, whether the insubstantial and the substantial can exchange, and whether the body can be centered and upright like a balanced scale all depend on the hips.

The waist and the hips are interrelated. People often call them the "waist-hips" because the hips must be mentioned when talking about the waist and the waist must be mentioned when talking about the hips.

The first thing one should do is to make the hips relaxed and open. The crotch can be rounded when the hips are relaxed and open—usually referred to as "open the hips and round the crotch." However, when we say "the hips should be relaxed and open," we are not saying that the hips should be spread apart. If the clearances between the bones at the hips are not opened through relaxation, the crotch will not be rounded even with the hips spread apart. With a rounded crotch, the spinning or rotating movements will be agile and the upper and lower body will be integrated.

Also, the hips should be relaxed and should make a good seat. If the hips make a good seat, the feet will be flat and firm on the ground. The feet will then naturally grasp the ground and qi will pass down to the soles, which makes one stand as stable as a mountain. There is a state where the hips seem "seated," but they actually are not. If you find that your feet cannot stay flat and firm on the ground, you should adjust your hips.

Furthermore, the hips should sink. Seating the hips is substantial, whereas sinking is insubstantial. If you can make the hips seated and sunken, you can also make them substantial and insubstantial at the same time, and be centered and upright. The weight is then tied to the hips, from where it transfers to the soles.

Bending of the knees depends on seating of the hips. If you can make the hips properly seated, you can naturally bend properly at the knees. You should absolutely not bend your knees without making the hips seated. The knees should only be bent to an extent depending on how much the hips are seated. To agilely rotate and move, the knees and the hips should be vertically aligned and adequate room for bending and extending should be reserved.

The knees should not be bent too much. The crotch or the buttocks positioned below the knee level and/or the knees moving beyond the toes are considered excessive. Excessive bending at the knees ruins the centered and upright state, makes the practitioner vulnerable, makes weight shifting difficult, exposes the knees to injury, hinders *qi* from passing to the soles, blocks the path of energy, and makes complete integration of *qi* impossible.

Briefly put, the centered and upright state actually means that "rather than the outer appearance, the spirit naturally gains a centered state." The *qi* of the Middle Jiao runs through the heart, kidneys, spine, and the bone marrow of the limbs. If the heart/mind and spirit are "centered and upright," the appearance of the body will not be tilted, the energy will be handled without excess or deficiency, and, moreover, even when the body tilts, it will be straight.

For example, in the "punching the ground" posture, the torso does tilt but a straight line is formed through the top of the head, back, leg, and foot. The *qi* of the Middle Jiao runs through from the top of the head to the foot as well, which maintains the centered and upright state even in a tilted posture. Therefore, centered and upright can be described as "when the whole body moves with exuberant *qi* at the core, even a form that appears slanted is governed by centered and upright *qi*." The centered and upright state can be automatically maintained if the upper and the lower body are penetrated by *qi* and the internal *qi* circulates as one. This fact should be taken as a rule in Taiji push-hands exercises.

2. Upper and lower body follow each other; the internal and the external combine into one

Taiji push-hands is an integrated movement of the entire body and the mind. It requires a high integration of intent, *qi*, spirit, and the body, and it also requires the body and the limbs to be in harmony with each other under the guidance of the brain. When one part moves, all parts move; when one part closes, all parts close. As a result, the internal energy of Taiji can penetrate all sections from the feet up to the legs, waist, spine, shoulders, and hands.

To meet the requirement of moving the whole body as one, when practicing, "the upper body and the lower body should follow each other, the internal and the external should combine into one, and *qi* should circulate throughout the body." Of course, a practitioner cannot enter this state overnight. It requires long-term and unremitting efforts and study. As in the proverb "more haste, less speed," a practitioner is not supposed to seek quick success.

The classics state that "when the upper and lower body follow each other, it is difficult for the opponent to invade," pointing out how effective and important the coordination between the upper and the lower body is. "The upper and the lower follow each other" means that the lower back is taken as the axis that connects the upper and lower body. The lower back "links the arms" and makes "the legs follow" (see below). When the upper body and the lower body follow each other, the middle body will follow naturally.

"Linking the arms" has two meanings: (1) the arms should be inter-linked; and (2) the arms should be linked with the legs. The intent is that when one part opens, all parts open; when one part closes, all parts close; and there is closing in opening and there is opening in closing.

Inter-linking the arms means that it is as if there is an invisible rubber band (intent and *qi*) between the shoulders, between the elbows, and between the hands. The band ties each pair together, links left and right, makes each pair symmetric, and creates attraction between the left and right side of each pair.

For example, when opening the arms, it feels difficult to open them, and when they are opened, the mind-intent and *qi* are not broken. When closing the arms, it feels difficult to close them, and when they are closed, there is no gap between yin and yang.

"The legs following" has two meanings: (1) the legs should follow each other; and (2) the lower body should follow when the upper body moves, and the movements of the lower body should be led by the upper body. The intent is that when the upper body is insubstantial, the lower body should be substantial; when the upper body is substantial, the lower body should be insubstantial; and insubstantial exists in substantial, and substantial exists in insubstantial.

That the legs follow each other means that when the left leg spirals clockwise, the right leg should spiral counterclockwise, and when the right leg spirals clockwise, the left should spiral counterclockwise. When the left leg bends like a bow, the right should extend, and when the right leg bends like a bow, the left should extend. When the left foot is substantial, the right should be insubstantial, and when the right foot is substantial, the left should be insubstantial. When the left hip is seated, the right should sink, and when the right hip is seated, the left should sink. When the left foot moves forward, the right should follow, and when the right foot moves forward, the left should follow. When the left foot moves backward, the right should follow, and when the right foot moves backward, the left should follow. When moving forward, the back is insubstantial, and when moving backward, the front is insubstantial. When the upper body moves, the lower should follow. When the lower body moves, the upper should take the lead, which means that the feet move following the hands, and the hands lead the feet to move; the upper and the lower combine into one and they rotate like a pearl.

The following serve as concrete examples of the above. When the arms are applying *peng* energy upward, the legs should tend to subside; when the arms are applying *lü* energy to the left and back, the left leg should spiral in the *shun* direction and the right leg in the *ni* direction following the hands; when the hands are applying *ji* energy forward, the front leg should bend like a bow and the rear leg press down with the foot; when the hands are applying *an* energy downward, the hips should be seated, the knees bent, and the body descended; and when a leg is to lift, it should be led by a hand.

"When the upper body and the lower body follow each other, the middle body will follow naturally" has two meanings: (1) when the upper and the lower body move, the middle body follows; and (2) when the middle body moves, the upper body and the lower body conform to it. The intent is that the hands, feet, chest, abdomen, waist, and spine move together and the hands, feet, and body arrive at the same time: "when one part moves, every part moves"; "the upper and the lower are penetrated by *qi*."

"When the upper and the lower body move, the middle body follows" means that the chest, abdomen, waist, and spine move to match the movements of the hands and the feet. In order to do so, it is crucial for the chest, abdomen, waist, and spine to be properly insubstantial/substantial, relaxed, agile, and centered and upright.

Let us use the *peng, lü, ji,* and *an* energies as examples. When the arms are applying *peng* upward, the legs should sink and the hips should be seated, and the chest and the abdomen will then open naturally. In that state, the upper is insubstantial and the lower is substantial. When the hands are applying *lü* to the right, the right leg should spiral to the *shun* direction, the left leg should spiral to the *ni* direction, the waist and spine should rotate to the right simultaneously, and *qi* should flow and circulate to both sides. When the hands are applying *ji* forward, the front leg should bend and the rear leg should press down with the foot, and the body should move forward. When the hands are applying *an* downward, the knees should bend, the hips should be seated, the chest and the abdomen conform to each other, the body sinks, and the energy of the waist penetrates downward.

"When the middle body moves, the upper body and the lower body conform to it" means that movement and neutralization happen entirely in the chest and the abdomen, and that rotation depends entirely on the waist and the spine. The key is to use the shoulder as an agile pivot point for the rotation of the arm, and to use the hip as an agile pivot point for the rotation of the leg. When the chest and abdomen open, the upper and the lower, as well as the limbs, open, and when the chest and abdomen close, the upper and the lower, as well as the limbs, close. When the torso moves forward, the upper and the lower move forward together, and when the torso moves backward, the upper and the lower both move backward. When the waist and the spine rotate, both the upper and the lower rotate.

In short, when the middle does not move, the upper and the lower will not move; when the middle moves, the upper and the lower move simultaneously and there is clear separation between yin and yang; the upper and the lower follow each other; opening and closing alternate; motion and stillness result in each other; bending and extending fit each other; insubstantial and substantial react to each other; left and right connect with each other; and internal and external conform to each other.

All parts of the body will make an integral whole in Taijiquan push-hands if the upper and the lower follow each other and the internal and the external combine into one. "All parts of the body make an integral whole" means that the upper segment, the middle segment, and the lower segment combine into one and intent, *qi*, and spirit merge into one. The integrated internal *qi* is guided by the mind/intent to pass through the upper and the lower. The *qi* circulates spirally, enters the bone marrow, emerges out of the bone clearances, fills the muscles and the skin, reaches the tips of the limbs, and flows along the meridians and throughout the entire body, integrating the whole body into one.

Based on the above, it should be evident that "the upper and the lower follow each other and the internal and external combine into one" describes another regulation for exercising Taiji push-hands.

3. Transformation between substantial and insubstantial, and turning from the waist

The waist is the controller of the entire body, the link between the upper and the lower body, and the axis of transformation between the left and the right. The waist, together with the hips, maintains the centered and upright state and the balance of the body. Together with the spine, the waist influences the flow of the *qi* of the Middle Jiao, the lowering of *qi* to the *dantian*, the inward and outward movement of the internal *qi*, and the insubstantiality of the upper body and the substantiality of the lower body.

Therefore, great importance has been attached to the state and role of the waist. It is said that "orders originate from the waist," and to "take care of the waist at every moment." In the Taiji classics, it reads: "Everything is dominated by the waist," "The rotation is done at the waist," "If you fail to gain adequate power, you must look to your waist and legs," and "The most crucial point is the movement and neutralization at the chest and waist." These all show the importance of the waist.

In Taiji push-hands, the transformation between insubstantial and substantial should be done by turning from the waist, which means that the overall state of insubstantial and substantial in the body is controlled by the waist. If insubstantial and substantial are distinguished clearly from each other at the waist, they will be distinguished everywhere in the body. If they are not distinguished at the waist, they will not be distinguished everywhere in the body.

"Insubstantial and substantial should be distinguished clearly from each other" actually means that the waist is the primary location where the distinction should be made. If there is double-heaviness at the waist, then double-heaviness will be everywhere in the body. The saying "The problem of double-heaviness has not been understood" actually means, first of all, that double-heaviness exists at the waist.

The waist is the controller of the entire body, because the waist is the key to the transformation between insubstantial and substantial in the torso, in the feet, and even in the hands. If insubstantial and substantial are distinguished clearly from each other, central equilibrium will result naturally.

The five steps, namely "forward," "backward," "beware of the left," "look to the right," and "central equilibrium," all have insubstantial and substantial in them. When moving forward, the rear is insubstantial; when withdrawing backward, the front is insubstantial; when "being wary of the left," the right is insubstantial; when "looking to the right," the left is insubstantial; and as for central equilibrium, equilibrium exists in the center of insubstantial and substantial.

For "transformation to happen in the waist," the waist should, first of all, be relaxed, sunk, and made insubstantial. If the waist is relaxed, sunk, and insubstantial, it will be adaptable. Adaptability will enable the waist to rotate, and rotation will make the waist agile.

The opposite of relaxed waist is compressed waist/lower back, which can be resolved by loosening and relaxing the inter-vertebral gaps and tendons. The opposite of sunk waist is concave lower back, which can be resolved by relaxing and sinking the waist and lower back (aided by restraining the buttocks). The opposite of insubstantial waist is a "corset waist." The waist should not be stiff or soft, but something in between, in order to be insubstantial and empty. Being insubstantial also means being empty. The compressed, concave, and corset waist are all caused by tension at the waist and are not acceptable in Taiji push-hands.

Relaxing the waist allows the abdomen to relax, and then the whole area can subsequently become relaxed and perfectly round, which will enable *qi* to lower to the *dantian* and run through the *dai* (belt) meridian. Provided that the hips are relaxed and sunk as well, and the crotch is arched, the energy of the waist will be able to thread down to empower the legs and *qi* will be able to descend to the soles to make the lower segment stable, making the upper body insubstantial and the lower body substantial.

In order to sink the waist, the buttocks must be tucked in. Being able to tuck in the buttocks should allow sinking of the waist. When the waist is sunk and the buttocks are tucked in, the coccyx (*weilü*) will be centered and vertical, the sacrum will be powerful, and the *mingmen* in the lumbar region will be relaxed and open naturally. The addition of lifting the *huiyin* and insubstantially leading the head upward will make the spine upright and straight and the *qi* of the Middle Jiao flow through inside the spine. The upper and the lower body will then be strung together, the energy will be in harmony in every direction, and changing energy without deviation will be effortless.

The transformation between insubstantial and substantial can be done through rotating at the waist. In Taiji push-hands, the weight is also transferred through rotation of the waist, instead of through movements "without rotation of the waist." It is important to distinguish between movements with rotation and without rotation.

Without rotating at the waist, insubstantial and substantial cannot be transformed into each other, the upper and the lower body cannot follow each other, silk-reeling of the whole body cannot be performed, and energy cannot be changed internally. In Taiji push-hands and fighting, without rotating at the waist, a practitioner cannot "guide the opponent to enter into emptiness," cannot adhere/connect/stick/follow, and cannot "give up oneself and follow the opponent." The practitioner will inevitably be in a passive position and controlled by the opponent all the time. Therefore, changing between insubstantial and substantial via rotating at the waist is another regulation of Taiji push-hands.

4. Three sections, four tips, five bows, and six harmonies

In the body techniques of Taijiquan, there are divisions into three sections, four tips, five bows, and six harmonies. For practicing push-hands, it is important to know what these divisions mean.

Three sections

The human body can be divided into three sections, namely the tip section, the middle section, and the root (base) section. Each of these three sections can be divided further into three subsections, also called the tip, middle, and root. So, there are altogether nine sections. They are listed as follows:

- The arm is the tip section. The hand is the tip subsection of the arm, the elbow is the middle subsection, and the shoulder is the root subsection. These are the three subsections of the arm, and they are also called the three tip subsections.

- The torso is the middle section. The head is the tip subsection of the torso, the chest is the middle subsection, and the lower *dantian* is the root subsection. These are the three subsections of the torso, and they are also called the three middle subsections.

- The leg is the root section. The foot is the tip subsection of the leg, the knee is the middle subsection, and the hip is the root subsection. These are the three subsections of the leg, and they are also called the three root subsections.

Each of the nine sections has a corresponding orifice:

- The three orifices for the three tip subsections: The *laogong* is the orifice for the tip subsection, the *quchi* is the orifice for the middle subsection, and the *jianjing* is the orifice for the root subsection.

- The three orifices for the three middle subsections: The upper *dantian* is the orifice for the tip subsection, the middle *dantian* is the orifice for the middle subsection, and the lower *dantian* is the orifice for the root subsection.

- The three orifices for the three root subsections: The *yongquan* is the orifice for the tip subsection, the *dubi* is the orifice for the middle subsection, and the *huantiao* is the orifice for the root subsection.

While practicing *gong*, the orifices on the meridians and collaterals are passed under the guidance of the mind/intent, and the body is relaxed section by section and threaded together section by section. Starting, following, and chasing are the main points when initiating movement, which means that the tip section starts to move, the middle section follows, and the root section chases. For instance, when the arms start to move, the torso follows and the legs chase; when the hands start to move, the elbows follow and the shoulders chase; and when the feet start to move, the knees follow and the hips chase.

Internal *qi* should be guided to run through the three sections, reach the four tips, distribute to the five elements, and fill in the nine orifices. The internal and external aspects, the upper and lower parts, the left and right sides, and the tip, middle, and root sections and subsections should all be threaded together section by section into one section. The integrated *qi* will enter the marrow, emerge from the gaps in the joints, pass through the *dantian*, the orifices, and the meridians and collaterals, and flow throughout the body.

Four tips

The four tips mean the four tips or ends in a human body. The hair is the end of blood; the fingers/toes are the ends of tendons (in hands/feet); the tongue is the end of flesh; and the teeth are the ends of bones. When all the four tips are activated simultaneously, the indicators are: the hair is about to lift the hat, the fingers/toes are about to penetrate bones, the tongue is about to break the teeth, and the teeth are about to cut through metal.

Moreover, the Heart (mind), the Gallbladder (courage), and *qi* should collaborate. When the mind starts to move, *qi* emerges from the *dantian*, the four tips activate simultaneously, the courage from the Gallbladder maintains steadiness, and the five elements will be in harmony. The classics tell us: "When *qi* emerges from the *dantian*, it is fierce and malicious like a tiger and alert like a dragon. When *qi* is emitted, a sound is made. The sound follows the hands, and the hands land on the opponent's body along with the sound. When one branch in a tree shakes, one hundred branches shake. When the four tips move at the same time, even the ghosts and gods will be afraid." The simultaneous activation of the four tips is considered to signal the activation *neigong* and mastery of *gongfu* in Taijiquan or Taiji push-hands.

Five bows

The five bows refer to the fact that, in the body, the torso should be like a bow, each arm should be like a bow, and each leg should be like a bow. Combining the five bows into one creates integrated whole-body energy: "Like a mountain when still; like a river when moving." The energy can be stored or emitted in constant surges. "The body is like a bow and the energy is like an arrow" means that the "five bows combine into one."

The waist is like the handle of the torso bow. The mind/intent should be always concentrated on the *mingmen* opposite to the navel. The *mingmen* should be in central equilibrium, without tilting or swaying. The *mingmen* should provide support from the back. The *yamen* (in the depression below the spinous process of the first cervical vertebra) and the *weilü* (coccyx) are just like the two symmetric ends of the bow, which adjust the movements and enhance the capacity of drawing and restoring.

The elbow is like the handle of the arm bow. The mind/intent should be concentrated on the elbows in order to make them relaxed, still, and fixed to one direction. The wrist and the collarbone beneath the neck are considered the two ends of the arm bow. The ends must be fixed and symmetric. The hands, when relaxed, soft, and agile, can be fixed through settling the wrists. The collarbones can be fixed by using the mind/intent so that they will neither tilt nor sway. The collarbone controls the directions of the hand movement, and therefore properly fixed collarbones are the prerequisite for fixing the hands.

The knee is like the handle of the leg bow. The hip bone and heel are considered the ends of the leg bow. The leg bow requires that the knee has power and sticks out a little; the hip is relaxed and sunk while providing support from the back; the heel sinks and energy rises; and the energy in the waist and legs follows and cooperates. "If there is a motion upward, there will be a motion downward; if there is a motion forward, there will be a motion backward; and if there is a motion leftward, there will be a motion rightward"—movements opposing and complementing each other, dragging each other and being symmetric, and allowing energy to be raised from the heels, controlled by the waist, passed through the back, and manifested through the fingers.

Among the five bows, the torso bow is the primary bow, whereas the arm bows and leg bows are complementary. The waist serves as the axis, the arms are tied to each other in the upper body, and the legs follow in the lower body. When the upper and the lower body follow each other, the middle body will follow. While practicing Taijiquan or Taiji push-hands, whenever changing a posture, it should be ensured that the five bows are formed and that the new posture is "supported in all directions."

Six harmonies

The three internal harmonies and the three external harmonies are referred to as the six harmonies.

What are the three internal harmonies? They are that the Heart/mind (*xin*) harmonizes with the intent (*yi*), the intent harmonizes with *qi*, and *qi* harmonizes with energy (*jin*). Moreover, when the Heart harmonizes with the eyes, the Spleen harmonizes with the muscles, the Lungs harmonize with the skin, the Kidneys harmonize with the bones, and the Liver harmonizes with the tendons, these are also called internal harmonies.

What are the three external harmonies? They are that the hands harmonize with the feet, the elbows harmonize with the knees, and the shoulders harmonize with the hips. Moreover, when the head harmonizes with the hands, the hands harmonize with the torso, and the torso harmonizes with the steps, these are also called external harmonies.

In short, the internal and the external should combine into one, the upper body and the lower body should follow each other, and the entire body should move in unison. As a result, an integral whole is formed.

B. HAND TECHNIQUES

Taijiquan theory states that "the hands follow the intent and express the techniques," pointing to the countless variety of hand techniques that can be employed in Taiji push-hands or fighting. However, as in the proverb "Nothing can be essentially different from the fundamentals despite all the apparent changes," all the hand techniques are composed of basic ones: the palm, the fist, and the hook.

1. Palm

Taiji push-hands and fighting make use of a great variety of palm (or open hand) techniques, including the flat palm, vertical palm, side palm, supporting palm, reverse palm, dropping palm, parting palms, folding palms, and yin–yang palms, among others. Mastering the basic principles of palm techniques is the key to mastering and using the palms. Mentioned below are some rules for exercising palm techniques. The basics of palm technique can be grasped by keeping the rules in mind.

For example, when the palms move forward, the shoulders should hasten the elbows, the elbows should hasten the hands, *qi* should penetrate the three sections to reach the tips, and intent, *qi*, power, form, and the internal and the external should combine into one. When the palms move from the left to the right or from the right to the left, the hands should lead the waist and the waist should drive the hands. When practicing pushing with palms and emitting energy, "the energy should rise from the feet, pass through the legs, run through the back, and reach the hands." The arms should be left slightly bent instead of letting them fully straighten in order to be able to react to changes and launch an attack.

There is an improper movement which should be avoided. The knee should not pass the toes or else the center of gravity will be lost and the centered and upright state cannot be kept.

2. Fist

In Taijiquan, a fist is formed in the same way as it is in other schools: the four fingers of an open hand are first closed one by one; then, led by the middle finger, the four fingers are clenched tighter; and finally the thumb is pressed on the middle section of the middle finger when the tip of the middle finger touches the center of the palm. The only difference between the Taijiquan fist and that of the other schools is that the Taijiquan fist is not supposed to be too tight. It should be relaxed, but not loose; and it should be properly tight, but not stiff. There should be an idea of gathering *qi* while making a fist.

When using the fist while emitting energy, the fist should be quickly clenched tight only at the moment it lands and then loosened immediately after. This technique aids in concentrating the energy on the fist while emitting energy and has the following three advantages:

- It contributes to the flowing back of *qi* to the *dantian*.

- It protects the fist and arm against seizing and joint-locking.

- Relaxing right after the impact makes it easier to defend against the opponent's possible counter-attack and to continue to fight.

3. Hook

The hook is a method to develop the strength of the wrist and fingers. In seizing and joint-locking techniques, it is applied for seizing. In Taiji push-hands and fighting technique, the hook is used to hold the opponent's vital parts, including the shoulders, elbows, hands, head, neck, waist, hips, knees, and feet to force the opponent to a dead angle or prevent the opponent from changing position.

The hook can be applied to grasp the tendons, hold the meridians, or jab the acupoints with the finger(s), thus blocking *qi* and cutting off energy. When seized with the hook, the opponent will be in too much pain to fight back. Combined with the techniques of beating, striking, and grappling, the seizing techniques using the hook hand can bring the power of Taiji push-hands and fighting into full play.

A practitioner skilled in applying the hook seizing techniques can control the speed, dynamics, and angle of the techniques. In push-hands or martial applications, the opponent's capacity should be taken into consideration in order to avoid accidental injuries.

All schools of Chinese martial arts elaborate on the subject of hook techniques to some degree. Taijiquan is, however, much more original in the research and application of the subject.

C. FOOTWORK TECHNIQUES

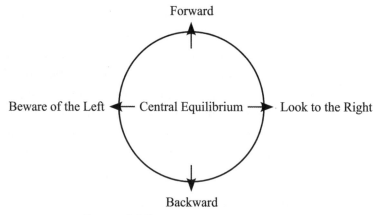

FIGURE 3.1 FIVE ELEMENTS FOOTWORK

Footwork and stances are the foundation of keeping balance, and if balance is unsteady, there must be a problem in one or both of these. Footwork refers to the various movements of the lower limbs as well as the fixed postures of balance. During push-hands or fighting, the footwork is the deciding factor in whether a practitioner is agile or clumsy. In Taiji theory, the role of footwork and stances is highlighted as: "Countless changes are made by me, owing to the foundation laid by my legs and feet."

Taiji push-hands and fighting technique requires that, when moving forward or backward, the legs mainly follow the hands. Insubstantial and substantial should be distinguished from each other, and the waist and the torso should follow the movement. When moving the feet to the left or the right, the hands mainly follow the feet. You should step along curves, and your feet should move with lightness and agility and land firmly. You must not be sloppy. When in central equilibrium or when making stationary changes, you should distinguish yin and yang, and insubstantial and substantial, clearly from each other. In order to maintain an insubstantial and agile state, you should never be overly solid.

In short, to guarantee that the torso is centered and upright and in balance, yin and yang should be distinguished and coordinated and the feet should not align with each other regardless of the stance. If these requirements are met, movement to any direction will be agile, steady, and relaxed. Convenient movement forward or backward, agility, steadiness, and centered and upright state should be regarded as the principles of footwork in Taiji push-hands and fighting.

The footwork of Taiji includes not only step forward, step backward, beware of the left, look to the right, and central equilibrium, but also techniques of dodging, jumping, and shifting. In a free fighting situation, both sides constantly make changes and apply various foot techniques and stances while trying to close in for an attack or move out of the way of an attack. Each side tries to get in an advantageous position.

Footwork and stances are of importance also because of the roles they play in forming postures, creating the conditions to attack, controlling the speeds of attack and defense, and winning over the necessary time to strive for victory. Body techniques, hand techniques, *neigong*, and speed, among others, can be brought into better play with clever and agile footwork.

Footwork should be combined with tactics. With flexible and varied footwork, you can move suddenly eastward and suddenly westward, abruptly forward and abruptly backward, seem to step forward but actually step backward, seem to step eastward but actually step westward, and mingling true with false and insubstantial with substantial. Thus the opponent will get confused and cannot judge your intention or utilize his tactics and techniques. The opponent will be in a muddle even before the attack is actually made.

Instead of applying footwork properly, some people just step back and forth. As a consequence, they often end up in a passive position.

"Step straight ahead in a favorable situation, step aside in an unfavorable situation," advises a proverb that provides a good example of the application of footwork in fighting. Therefore, in our daily practice, we should pay close attention to our footwork and stances. The application of footwork, that is, moving in the four main directions and staying in central equilibrium, dodging, shifting, jumping, and landing, should all have proper timing.

Additionally, we should try to apply the rule, "When the opponent does not move, I do not move; when the opponent is about to move, I move first," to footwork. If we can cleverly integrate foot techniques to match the situation by creating combinations from the attack and defense patterns in Taiji push-hands and fighting technique, we will be able to utilize the optimum routes for attack or defense. Thus, we will be quick when we attack, timely when we withdraw, and agile when we dodge. We will never be defeated because of the wide variety of our foot techniques.

1. The main footwork patterns in Taiji push-hands and fighting

1. Step forward (*jin bu*): A foot technique usually applicable to an attack. (Figure 3.2)

FIGURE 3.2

2. Step backward (*tui bu*): A foot technique applicable particularly to the protection of one's own weak points and the tactic of defending for attacking. (Figure 3.3)

FIGURE 3.3

3. Front bow stance (*qian gong bu*): A foot technique applied when emitting energy to attack. (Figure 3.4)

FIGURE 3.4

4. Sitting stance (*hou zuo bu*): A foot technique applied usually while neutralizing and shifting from defense to attack. (Figure 3.5)

FIGURE 3.5

5. Following step (*gen bu*): A foot technique applied to following quickly when there is an opening in the opponent's guard, used to "step straight ahead in a favorable situation." (Figure 3.6)

FIGURE 3.6

6. Empty stance (also called cat stance) (*xu bu*): A foot technique characterized by its clear separation of insubstantial and substantial and quickness in transforming into other stances, usually applied when "moving ahead or back, being wary of the left, or looking to the right." (Figure 3.7)

FIGURE 3.7

7. Switch step (*huan bu*): A foot technique applied to, via changing the positions of the feet, adjusting the center of gravity to obtain steadiness and make the body remain centered and upright. (Figures 3.8a, b)

FIGURE 3.8A   FIGURE 3.8B

8. Single leg stance (*duli bu*): A foot technique where the upper and the lower cooperate with each other to attack. (Figure 3.9)

FIGURE 3.9

9. Crouch stance (*pu bu*): A foot technique employed to attack the lower segment of the opponent. (Figure 3.10)

FIGURE 3.10

10. Circular step (*rao bu*): A foot technique characterized by "staying clear of the opponent's main force and striking at his weak points" and "fostering strengths and circumventing weaknesses," usually applied to the attack in a roundabout way. (Figures 3.11a, b)

FIGURE 3.11A   FIGURE 3.11B

11. Evading jump (*shang cuan bu*): A foot technique used for evading a blocking or sweeping leg of the opponent. (Figure 3.12)

FIGURE 3.12

12. Leaping step (*tiao yue bu*): Usually applied to getting over obstacles or in pursuit. (Figure 3.13)

FIGURE 3.13

2. Points for attention

- The feet should not be on the same front-to-back line; otherwise falling to the left side or right will be likely. (Figure 3.14)

FIGURE 3.14

- The feet should not be transversely parallel to each other; otherwise falling to the front or back will be likely. (Figure 3.15)

FIGURE 3.15

- The knee in the substantial leg should not be allowed to go beyond the toes (except in special cases); otherwise leaning forward will be likely. (Figure 3.16)

FIGURE 3.16

- The thighs of both legs should not be lower than the knees, or the energy will easily be broken; both legs should not be over-heavy and solid, or "double-heaviness" will easily result. (Figure 3.17)

FIGURE 3.17

D. EYE TECHNIQUES

Relying on the eyes, a practitioner can learn the opponent's status, seize the opportunity for attack, and vanquish the opponent. The eyes have long been called "the window of the heart." All the thoughts, emotions, and planned actions of the opponent are revealed by his eyes.

There are a lot of sayings about the eyes, including: "The heart/mind acts as a commander, the eyes as vanguards, the ears as scouts, the feet as a war horse, and the hands as weapons," and "The eyes watch six ways and the ears listen to eight directions." These sayings emphasize the key role played by the eyes. Moreover, a well-trained martial artist often deters the opponent psychologically with his imposing presence and sharp expression of the eyes.

In Taijiquan push-hands and fighting, the exchange of expressions in the eyes between the two sides is actually a psychological combat. It depends on the psychological strength of a martial artist to bring his skills into full play in a fight.

A martial artist will be able to lull and tempt the opponent, control the pace of the game, attack where the opponent is less guarded, and gain victory if he has good psychological strength and if he can use eye techniques in employing techniques and tactics. He can mingle true with false and substantial with insubstantial, hit the lower body while looking at the upper body and hit the right side while looking at the left side, and attack in the west while making a feint to the east.

Chapter IV

Silk-Reeling Exercises for All Parts of the Body

A. HEAD

1. Turning the head

Movements: Start with the *wuji* commencing posture, the feet shoulder-width apart. Keep the head upright, the shoulders level, and the body naturally relaxed. Look forward. Then gently rotate the head alternately to the left and right at a slow and uniform speed. Breathe naturally. (Figures 4.1, 4.2; see also Section A in Chapter V for a full description of the *wuji* posture)

FIGURE 4.1

FIGURE 4.2

Point for concentration: The upper *dantian*, at the *zuqiao* point between the eyebrows. (Figure 4.3)

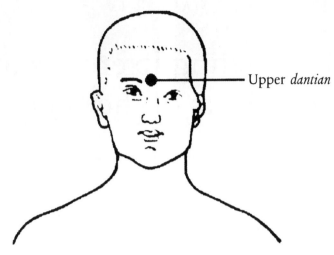

Upper dantian

FIGURE 4.3 THE ZUQIAO

Efficacy: Refreshes the brain, comforts the spirit, and improves the blood circulation in the brain and the blood's ability to provide oxygen.

Advice: Practitioners suffering from high blood pressure, dizziness, or headache are advised not to concentrate on the upper *dantian*. They should just do the rotating movements without concentration. If there is an uncomfortable feeling even when practicing the movements without concentration, the exercise should not be done at all.

The position of the head is the key to developing one's Taiji push-hands techniques and to keeping the "gravity line" of the body centered and straight. Keeping the head in a correct position makes it possible to prevent one from bowing forward, leaning backward, or slanting to the sides. Also, it brings the balance control of the body into full play.

2. Circling the neck

Movements: Start with the *wuji* commencing posture, the feet shoulder-width apart. Roll the head clockwise around the neck. The movement should be slow and uniform and the upper body should follow the movement of the head. Breathe naturally. (Figures 4.4, 4.5) Do further repetitions and then change the direction to counterclockwise.

FIGURE 4.4

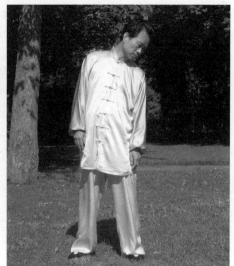

FIGURE 4.5

Point for concentration: The *dazhui*, located in the pit under the seventh cervical vertebra on the central line of the back. (Figure 4.6)

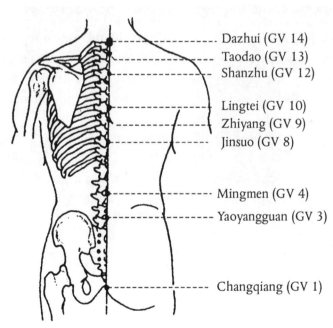

Dazhui (GV 14)
Taodao (GV 13)
Shanzhu (GV 12)

Lingtei (GV 10)
Zhiyang (GV 9)
Jinsuo (GV 8)

Mingmen (GV 4)
Yaoyangguan (GV 3)

Changqiang (GV 1)

FIGURE 4.6 THE *DAZHUI*

Efficacy: Regular exercise promotes the relaxation of the neck, increases the range of motion of the neck, promotes the agility and flexibility of the neck in order to "rotate at a touch," improves the ability of the neck to bear strikes, and improves the circulation of *qi* and blood in the neck. Furthermore, the exercise is particularly effective in easing neck ache, muscle rigidity, spur, stiff neck, and shortage of blood or oxygen supply to the neck, among others.

Advice: The upper body follows the rotation of the neck, but it should not tilt forward or lean backward too much.

B. UPPER LIMBS

1. Circling the shoulders

Movements: Start with the *wuji* commencing posture, the feet shoulder-width apart. Clench the hands into hollow fists and put them on the sides of the body. Slowly lower your weight by gradually bending the legs. At the same time, hollow the chest and drop the shoulders. (Figures 4.7, 4.8)

FIGURE 4.7   FIGURE 4.8

Rising up, push out the chest and make a circle with the shoulders by first moving them upward and then backward, downward, and forward. Bend the elbows following the circling movement. Breathe naturally. After doing further repetitions, reverse the direction. (Figure 4.9)

FIGURE 4.9

Point for concentration: The *jianjing*, at the midpoint between the *dazhui* and the acromion (the highest point of the shoulder). (Figure 4.10)

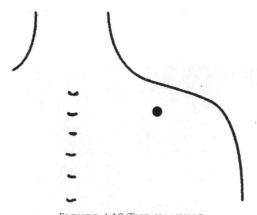

FIGURE 4.10 THE *JIANJING*

Efficacy: Regular practice of the silk-reeling exercise of the shoulders is good for relaxing the shoulders and increasing the shoulder rotation range of the motion. It improves the agility of the shoulder to "rotate at a touch" and change the direction of a force. It improves the effectiveness of the shoulder's actions in neutralizing incoming energy (*jin*) or emitting energy and also the practitioner's ability to bear strikes. Furthermore, it improves the *qi* and blood circulation of the shoulders and is effective in helping to treat omarthritis, omalgia, and motor impairment of the arm.

Moreover, the exercise can enlarge the capacity of the bones for bearing force, strengthen the tendons, improve the stability of the joints, and increase the range of movement of the shoulders. Also, the exercise promotes the secretion of bone fluid and lubricates and nurtures the joints and cartilages. Practicing the exercise can slow down osteoporosis and prevent the joints from being prematurely aged. It may ease muscle stiffness and make the muscles more flexible and elastic. The exercise may improve the ability of the local systems to circulate the lymph, blood, and *qi*, which is good for the metabolism and absorption of nutrients.

Advice: The silk-reeling exercises for each part of the body all have the above-mentioned effects. Silk-reeling exercises of the shoulders include single-shoulder and single-arm exercises in addition to the one described above.

2. Opening and closing silk-reeling of the elbows

Movements: Start with the *wuji* commencing posture. Move the feet a little bit wider than shoulder-width apart. Bend the knees and lower your weight. At the same time, hollow the chest and tuck the stomach in. Clench the fingers into fists and bring the hands together in front of the stomach. (Figures 4.11, 4.12)

FIGURE 4.11   FIGURE 4.12

Then part the arms by circling the elbows from the front upward, then backward and downward, completing a full circle. Raise and lower the center of gravity along with the movement of the elbows. Breathe naturally. Do further repetitions and then reverse the direction.

Point for concentration: The *quchi*, at the lateral end of the transverse cubital crease of a flexed elbow. (Figure 4.13)

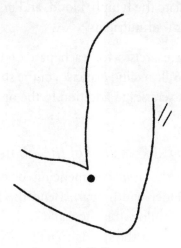

FIGURE 4.13 THE *QUCHI*

Efficacy: Regular practice of the silk-reeling exercise of the elbows is good for relaxing the elbows and increasing the elbow rotation range of the motion. It improves the agility of the elbow to "rotate at a touch" and change the direction of a force. It improves the effectiveness of the elbow's actions in neutralizing incoming energy (*jin*) or emitting energy and also the practitioner's ability to bear strikes. Furthermore, it improves the *qi* and blood circulation of the elbows and is effective in helping to treat elbow pain, arthritis, and motor impairment of the arm.

Advice: A Taijiquan proverb asserts that "the elbow never touches the costal area," so a distance of one fist or so between the elbow and the ribs should be kept while practicing. In addition to this exercise, the silk-reeling exercises for the elbows include single-elbow exercises as well as fixed-direction exercises to the front, back, left, and right.

3. Circling the hands

Movements: Start with the *wuji* commencing posture, the feet shoulder-width apart. Raise both arms slowly to the front. Make a circle with both hands from the inside to outside around the wrists. Breathe naturally. Do further repetitions and then reverse the direction. (Figures 4.14, 4.15)

FIGURE 4.14   FIGURE 4.15

Point for concentration: The *laogong*, at the center of the palm, between the second and the third metacarpal bones, but closer to the third. Touched by the tip of the third finger when the fingers are clenched into a fist. (Figure 4.16)

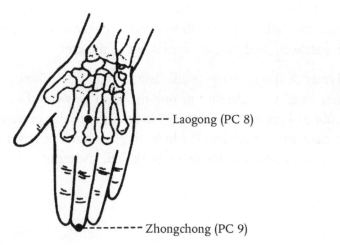

FIGURE 4.16 THE *LAOGONG* AND *ZHONGCHONG*

Efficacy: Regular practice of the silk-reeling exercise of the wrists is good for relaxing the wrists and increasing the wrist rotation range of the motion. It improves the agility of the wrist to "rotate at a touch" and change the direction of a force. It improves the effectiveness of the wrist's actions in neutralizing incoming energy (*jin*) or emitting energy and also the practitioner's ability to bear strikes, and promotes the seizing and joint-locking techniques. Furthermore, it improves the *qi* and blood circulation of the hands and wrists.

The *laogong* on the hand is an important acupoint in Qigong. The hand is the place where the three yang meridians of the hand and the three yin meridians of the hand originate and link. The concentration on the *laogong* combined with a spiral twining movement of the hand in this silk-reeling exercise can be effective in helping *qi* reach the tip section of the hand and make *qi* flow smoothly along the six meridians of the hand.

Advice: The silk-reeling exercises for the wrists include single-hand exercises in addition to this exercise.

4. Spiral silk-reeling to the left and right with the arms

Movements: Start with the *wuji* commencing posture. Take a large step to the left with the left foot, leaving the weight on the right foot. Inhale and make a clockwise circle on the front-left side of the body with the left hand. Let the hand lead the movement of the arm. Exhale and move the left hand downward, keeping it close to the left side of the chest, and then, with the palm facing upward, continue the movement along the left leg all the way down to the instep of the left foot. (Figures 4.17, 4.18)

FIGURE 4.17   FIGURE 4.18

After that, shift your weight to the left foot. Inhale and make a counterclockwise circle on the front-right side of the body with the right hand. Let the hand lead the movement of the arm. Exhale and move the right hand downward, keeping it close to the right side of the chest, and then, with the palm facing upward, continue the movement along the right leg all the way down to the instep of the right foot. Do further repetitions of the exercise. (Figures 4.19, 4.20)

FIGURE 4.19

FIGURE 4.20

Point for concentration: The *laogong*.

Efficacy: Improves the overall attack and defense capabilities of the arms through the actions of "when intent arrives, *qi* arrives; when *qi* arrives, movement arrives; the internal and external combine into one; and *qi* threads through three sections."

Advice: The silk-reeling exercises for the arms also include single-arm exercises for the left and the right arm, double-armed smooth and reverse silk-reeling, smooth and reverse silk-reeling for the left and right single arm, double-armed diagonal opening and closing silk-reeling, and double-armed front/back and up/down spiral silk-reeling.

C. TORSO

1. Rotating the chest

Movements: Start with the *wuji* commencing posture. Make a step forward with the right foot and shift the weight to the right foot. Rotate the left half of the chest backward and shift the weight onto the left foot. The left arm and the waist follow the movement. Breathe naturally. Do further repetitions and then change the left foot to front and do the exercise from the other side. (Figures 4.21, 4.22, 4.23)

FIGURE 4.21   FIGURE 4.22

FIGURE 4.23

Point for concentration: The *danzhong*, on the midline of the sternum, at the level of the fourth intercostal space. (Figure 4.24)

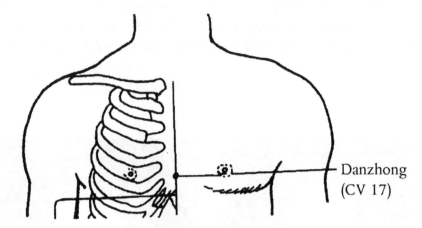

FIGURE 4.24 THE *DANZHONG*

Efficacy: Improves the agility of the chest to "rotate at a touch" and redirect force. It improves the effectiveness of the chest's actions in neutralizing incoming energy or emitting energy and also the practitioner's ability to bear strikes, and promotes the seizing and joint-locking techniques. Furthermore, it improves the *qi* and blood circulation in the chest.

The *danzhong* point is right at the center of the chest, the position where all yin meridians meet, so it is considered an important acupoint in Qigong. Concentrating on the *danzhong* will help *qi* in the yin meridians and the five Zang-organs to flow smoothly, enabling the five Zang-organs to function well.

Advice: The Heart and the Lungs are located in the center of the chest. The Heart dominates the blood, the Lungs dominate *qi*, and they power the circulation of *qi* and blood in the entire body. Rotation of the chest causes opening and closing in the chest that enlarges the thoracic cavity and increases the capacity of the Lungs. At the same time, it lessens the pressure on the Heart and improves the function of the Heart.

2. Abdomen

Movements: Start with the *wuji* commencing posture, the feet shoulder-width apart. Let the hands drop naturally. Keep the eyes half-closed, look inwards at the middle *dantian*, and make the three *xing* (eyes, ears, heart) merge into one. After standing still and concentrating for a short while, the hands lead the abdomen to make a circle from the right to the left. The center of gravity follows the movement and shifts between the legs. Do further repetitions and then reverse the direction. (Figures 4.25, 4.26)

FIGURE 4.25   FIGURE 4.26

Point for concentration: The middle *dantian*. (Figure 4.27)

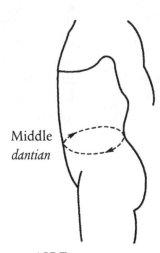

Middle
dantian

FIGURE 4.27 THE MIDDLE *DANTIAN*

Efficacy: Improves the agility of the abdomen to "rotate at a touch" and redirect force. It improves the effectiveness of the abdomen's actions in neutralizing incoming energy or emitting energy and also the practitioner's ability to bear strikes, and promotes the seizing and joint-locking techniques. Furthermore, it improves the *qi* and blood circulation in the abdomen.

The middle *dantian* is a fundamental point in Qigong practice. When the concentration on the *dantian* using the "three *xing* merge into one" method and the rotation of the abdomen are coordinated and reach a certain degree, *qi* can be felt flowing like water in the middle *dantian*, following the movement of the abdomen. After accumulating over a long period, *qi* will form a globular *dan* which rotates following the rotation of the abdomen. The practitioner can then approach the state of "the internal and the external combine into one."

Advice: The rotating movements of the abdomen have a massaging action that promotes peristalsis of the stomach, improving digestion, absorption, and metabolism.

3. Rotating the spine

Movements: Start with the *wuji* commencing posture. Move the feet a little bit wider than shoulder-width apart. Rotate the body alternately to the left and back and to the right and back. Let the arms swing following the rotation of the body and shift the center of gravity with the movement as well. (Figures 4.28, 4.29)

FIGURE 4.28   FIGURE 4.29

Point for concentration: The *shenzhu*, below the spinous process of the third thoracic vertebra. (Figure 4.30)

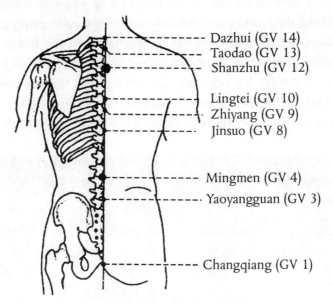

Dazhui (GV 14)
Taodao (GV 13)
Shanzhu (GV 12)

Lingtei (GV 10)
Zhiyang (GV 9)
Jinsuo (GV 8)

Mingmen (GV 4)
Yaoyangguan (GV 3)

Changqiang (GV 1)

FIGURE 4.30 THE *SHENZHU*

Efficacy: Beneficial for relaxing the spinal joints and increasing the spinal rotation range of the motion. Improves the agility of the spine to "rotate at a touch" and change the direction of a force. It improves the effectiveness of the spine's actions in neutralizing incoming energy or emitting energy and also the practitioner's ability to bear strikes. Furthermore, it improves the *qi* and blood circulation of the spine and is effective in helping to treat deficiency of Kidney *qi*, pain in the lower back, muscular strain in the lower back, and the protrusion of the intervertebral discs.

Advice: When rotating the spine, the muscles contract and spiral up and down, and as a result, it may feel as if "the spine is threaded together segment by segment, *qi* adheres to the back, and force is emitted from the spine." The exercise of Taiji push-hands creates a centrifugal force through the rotation of the waist and drives the internal energy to flow to the four tips. It should be pointed out that the feeling mentioned above requires reaching the state of "three *xing* merge into one."

Owing to the concentration needed in practicing the exercise, the feeling of "*qi* condenses into the bones and marrow" will come into being gradually. Furthermore, the nervous system will be adjusted and the physique strengthened.

4. Rotating the waist

Movements: Start with the *wuji* commencing posture. Move the feet a little bit wider than shoulder-width apart. Bend the knees and lower the center of gravity. Bend the elbows and raise the arms forward, leaving a distance of 80cm between the arms. Clench the fingers and turn the hands so that the eyes of the fists (palmar side) face each other. Rotate alternately to the left and right so that the waist is guided by the fists and the fists are guided by the waist. Meanwhile, the eyes should follow the direction of the fists. Breathe naturally. Do further repetitions of the movement. (Figures 4.31, 4.32)

FIGURE 4.31   FIGURE 4.32

Point for concentration: The *mingmen*, below the spinous process of the second lumbar vertebra. (Figure 4.33)

Efficacy: Beneficial for relaxing the waist and increasing the waist rotation range of the motion. Improves the agility of the waist to "rotate at a touch" and change the direction of a force. It improves the effectiveness of the waist's actions in neutralizing incoming energy or emitting energy and also the practitioner's ability to bear strikes. Furthermore, it improves the *qi* and blood circulation of the waist and is effective in helping to treat deficiency of Kidney *qi*, pain in the lower back, muscular strain in the lower back, and the protrusion of the intervertebral discs.

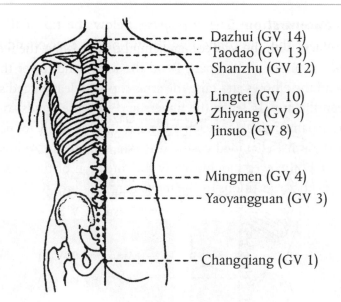

Dazhui (GV 14)
Taodao (GV 13)
Shanzhu (GV 12)

Lingtei (GV 10)
Zhiyang (GV 9)
Jinsuo (GV 8)

Mingmen (GV 4)
Yaoyangguan (GV 3)

Changqiang (GV 1)

FIGURE 4.33 THE *MINGMEN*

5. Circling the buttocks

Movements: Start with the *wuji* commencing posture, the feet shoulder-width apart. Bend at the knees. Circle the buttocks, starting from the left by first moving upward, right, and then downward. The center of gravity of the body shifts to the left and right following the movement. Do further repetitions and then reverse the direction. (Figures 4.34, 4.35)

FIGURE 4.34   FIGURE 4.35

Point for concentration: The *changqiang*, below the tip of the coccyx, at the midpoint of the line connecting the tip of the coccyx and the anus. (Figure 4.36)

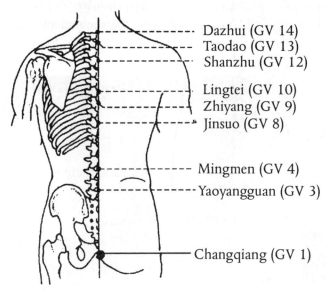

Dazhui (GV 14)
Taodao (GV 13)
Shanzhu (GV 12)

Lingtei (GV 10)
Zhiyang (GV 9)
Jinsuo (GV 8)

Mingmen (GV 4)
Yaoyangguan (GV 3)

Changqiang (GV 1)

FIGURE 4.36 THE *CHANGQIANG*

Efficacy: Improves the effectiveness of the buttocks' actions in neutralizing incoming energy or emitting energy and also the practitioner's ability to bear strikes. Furthermore, it improves the *qi* and blood circulation in the buttocks.

Advice: The buttocks tend to protrude slightly because of their physiological structure. If they protrude too much while practicing Taiji push-hands, the lower back will arch and the head will droop. Therefore, Taijiquan practitioners are required to tuck the buttocks in. The exercise of circling the buttocks is good for "tucking the buttocks in" and "descending *qi* to the *dantian.*"

D. LOWER LIMBS

1. Circling the hips

Movements: Start with the *wuji* commencing posture, the feet shoulder-width apart. Bend the knees. Rotate the hips counterclockwise in a horizontal circle. Let the center of gravity shift with the movement. Breathe naturally. Do further repetitions and then reverse the direction. (Figures 4.37, 4.38)

FIGURE 4.37   FIGURE 4.38

Point for concentration: The *huantiao*, at the junction of the lateral third and medial third of the line connecting the prominence of the greater trochanter and the sacral hiatus. (Figure 4.39)

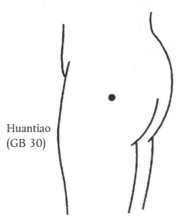

Huantiao
(GB 30)

FIGURE 4.39 THE *HUANTIAO*

Efficacy: Beneficial for relaxing the hip joints and increasing the hip rotation range of motion. It improves the agility of the hips to "rotate at a touch" and change the direction of a force. It improves the effectiveness of the waist's actions in neutralizing incoming energy or emitting energy and also the practitioner's ability to bear strikes. Furthermore, it improves the *qi* and blood circulation in the hips.

Advice: The hips are crucial in adjusting the waist and the legs, and the transfer from the legs to the waist happens through the hips. If the hips are not relaxed, the waist and the legs will not follow each other smoothly. When the waist turns, the hips connectively rotate. So, in fact, the turning of the waist means the rotation of the hips.

2. Silk-reeling with the knees

Movements: Start with the *wuji* commencing posture. Move the feet side by side and bend the knees to a half-squat posture. Place the hands on the knees and circle the knees clockwise horizontally. Breathe naturally. Do further repetitions and then reverse the direction. (Figures 4.40, 4.41)

FIGURE 4.40

FIGURE 4.41

Point for concentration: The *dubi*, at the lower border of the patella, in the depression lateral to the patella ligament, when the knee is flexed. (Figure 4.42)

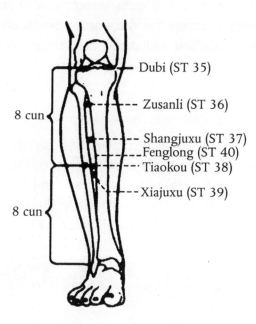

FIGURE 4.42 THE *DUBI*

Efficacy: Beneficial for relaxing the knee joints and increasing the knee rotation range of the motion. Improves the agility of the knees to "rotate at a touch" and change the direction of a force. It improves the effectiveness of the knees' actions in neutralizing incoming energy or emitting energy and also the practitioner's ability to bear strikes. Furthermore, it improves the *qi* and blood circulation of the knees and is effective in helping to treat pain in the knee and arthritis.

Advice: The legs support the weight of the entire body and the knees play an important role in supporting the body and in moving. To keep the knees agile and strong, and to keep the body centered and upright, the knees should not go beyond the toes (except in some special movements).

The silk-reeling exercises for the knees also include the single-knee circling exercises for the left and the right knee and the single-knee silk-reeling exercises for the left and the right knee.

3. Rotating the feet

Movements: Start with the *wuji* commencing posture, the feet shoulder-width apart. Shift the center of gravity onto the right foot with its toes pointing inward. Take the right heel as the axis and rotate the right foot so that the toes point outward. Breathe naturally. Do further repetitions and then do the exercise with the left foot. (Figures 4.43, 4.44)

FIGURE 4.43   FIGURE 4.44

Point for concentration: The *yongquan*, on the sole, in the depression that forms when the foot is in plantar flexion, approximately at the junction of the anterior third and posterior two-thirds of the sole. (Figure 4.45)

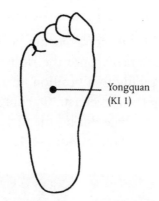

Yongquan
(KI 1)

FIGURE 4.45 THE *YONGQUAN*

Efficacy: Beneficial for relaxing the ankle joints and increasing the ankle rotation range of the motion. Improves the agility of the ankles to "rotate at a touch" and change the direction of a force. It improves the effectiveness of the ankles' actions in neutralizing incoming energy or emitting energy and also the practitioner's ability to bear strikes. Furthermore, it improves the *qi* and blood circulation of the ankles.

The *yongquan* is an important acupoint in Qigong. The foot is the place where the three yang meridians of the foot and the three yin meridians of the foot originate and link. The concentration on the *yongquan* can be effective in helping *qi* reach the tip section of the foot and make *qi* flow smoothly along the six meridians of the foot.

Advice: The feet, when forming stances, implementing footwork, and functioning as a support mechanism, are the foundation of the whole body. Nimbleness or tardiness of movement entirely depends on how effectively the footwork is performed. In Taiji push-hands, supporting and regulating the balance status of the whole body is done with footwork. Therefore, practicing silk-reeling of the feet is very important.

4. Legs

Movements: Start with the *wuji* commencing posture. Let the hands hang loosely. Shift the center of gravity onto the right foot. Bend the left knee and raise the left leg up spirally to a position next to the right knee. Look left-forward. Inhale during the movement. Opening from the hips, kick left-forward with the left heel. Exhale during the kick. Then perform the same movement with the right leg. (Figures 4.46–4.49)

FIGURE 4.46

FIGURE 4.47

FIGURE 4.48

FIGURE 4.49

Point for concentration: The *yongquan*.

Efficacy: When intent arrives, *qi* arrives; when *qi* arrives, physical force arrives; and *qi* penetrates the three sections. This exercise is especially effective for arthritis and for symptoms of coldness and leg and foot pain. It also increases the range of motion of the leg and makes the legs more effective in attack or defense.

Advice: The rotational and arched movements of the leg can be used as fighting techniques to block or hook the opponent's leg or foot and to stamp the opponent's knee or shank.

A Taijiquan proverb states that "*qi* flows like a crooked chain with nine pearls." The nine pearls refer to the neck, spine, lower back, shoulder, elbow, hand, hip, knee, and foot. (Figure 4.50)

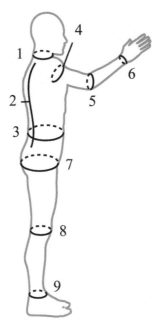

FIGURE 4.50 A CROOKED CHAIN WITH NINE PEARLS

—— CHAPTER V ——

Exercises of Taiji Neigong

Taijiquan belongs to the internal school (*neijia*) of boxing which pays special attention to the cultivation of *neigong* (internal power or skill). *Neigong* is regarded as the foundation of Taiji push-hands, and it should be developed all along the way from the beginner to the advanced levels of skill. The following proverbs emphasize its importance: "Exercise boxing without exercising *gong*, and you will get nothing in the end"; "Strength cannot match technique; technique cannot match *gong*." Therefore, the key in exercising Taiji push-hands and developing *gongfu* is to "grasp the *dantian* to cultivate *neigong*."

The substance of *neigong* is in the intent (*yi*) and *qi* conforming to each other and the spirit (*shen*) and *qi* combining with each other. The material foundation of *neigong* consists of the essence (*jing*), *qi*, and the spirit. One's level of *neigong* depends on one's quality of these three.

The starting point for improving one's *neigong* should be with the cultivation and strengthening of the essence, *qi*, and the spirit. If the essence is sufficient, *qi* will be sufficient; if *qi* is sufficient, the spirit will be vigorous; and if the spirit is vigorous, the physique will be perfect.

When exercising for health and self-defense, a practitioner should focus on health—"to cultivate one's *gongfu*" has this connotation. All *qi* should return to the root, that is, the *dantian*. This advice is the "secret of success" in cultivating the *dantian*.

"Grasp the *dantian* to cultivate *neigong*" means that, led by the mind, opening and closing, gathering and emitting, and exiting and entering happen at the *dantian*. When intending to open, which signifies motion, *qi* moves from the *dantian* to the four limbs; when intending to close, which indicates stillness, *qi* returns to the *dantian* from the four extremities; when moving forward, *qi* rushes to the navel from the *mingmen*; when moving backward, *qi* is pulled from the navel to the *mingmen*; when turning left, the *dantian* rotates to the left along the *dai* meridian; when turning right, the *dantian* rotates to the right along the *dai* meridian; and when staying in central equilibrium, the three *dantian*, including the upper *dantian*, the middle *dantian*, and the lower *dantian*, are penetrated by the *qi* of the Middle Jiao. The silk-reeling spirals throughout the body should conform to the rotation of the *dantian*.

To cultivate the *dantian*, a practitioner should learn how to conserve and replenish his energy. Priority should be given to conserving and replenishing *qi*, essence, and spirit. A whole decade should be spent on developing *gong*, and a decade spent on developing *gong* is also a decade spent on conserving and replenishing *qi*. "Simply cultivate *qi*, it can do you no harm." After a long period of practice, the genuine *qi* will be developed.

The spirit will be sufficient if *qi* is sufficient; longevity will be promoted if the spirit is sufficient. When the mind is still, the spirit arrives, and when the mind is moving, the spirit leaves. When the heart/mind (*xin*) is quiescent, then the spirit is in peace. A quiescent heart/mind conserves and replenishes the spirit.

Therefore, during the *neigong* exercises, the mind should be quiescent. Only if the mind is quiescent can essence, *qi*, and spirit be conserved, and only then can *neigong* be developed to a state where "three *xing* combine into one."

When learning to cultivate *neigong*, movements should be slow rather than quick. When the movements are slow, *qi* can be nourished. When doing the exercises of cultivating *neigong*, a practitioner should start with *wuji*, move slowly during the exercise, and finally close the exercise with a closing movement and then quietly stop moving. The exercises should be gentle, slow, calm, and steady, like a murmuring stream or a spring breeze. Each move and each posture should be done at a slow speed regardless of whether it is an opening and stretching movement, contracting and closing movement, or raising and/or lowering movement.

In short, a practitioner should keep his mind quiescent and motions slow in order to induce the internal *qi* to flow slowly throughout the body. The intent should be integrated with *qi* and the spirit integrated with the form, and then, following a natural course, the realm of forgetting both self and the outside world can be reached.

After having cultivated rich and full internal *qi* in the *dantian*, a practitioner may feel that a spheroid in the abdomen surges back and forth following the movements of emitting energy in Taiji push-hands. When moving slowly, the sphere rotates slowly; when moving fast, the sphere rotates quickly. When the sphere rotates inward, the practitioner "guides the opponent to enter into emptiness." When the sphere rotates outward, the practitioner attacks. A rotation of the sphere simultaneously contains both "guiding the opponent to enter into emptiness" and an attack.

It can be said that there is neutralization within emission and emission within neutralization, and that each motion "draws" a diagram of Taiji. It is impossible for a practitioner to enter into the advanced realm in which the internal and the external combine into one until his *neigong* reaches the standard mentioned above.

A. PREPARATORY EXERCISES

1. Wuji commencing posture

Stand with your feet parallel and shoulder-width apart. The neck should be straight and the head upright with the *baihui* point lifted towards the sky. The eyelids should be lowered and eye-sight turned inwards. The mouth should be closed so that the upper and lower teeth slightly touch and the lips are gently closed. The tip of the tongue should touch the upper palate. The shoulders should be relaxed and dropped, and the armpits should be kept hollow. The elbows should be dropped and the arms hung down naturally with the elbows slightly flexed. The chest should be "sucked in" to make it slightly concave, and the back should be stretched upwards. The waist should be relaxed and the hips loosened with the tailbone slightly tucked under. The knees should be slightly bent. The entire body should be relaxed. Breathing should be natural. Distracting thoughts should be dispelled, and the mind should be clear and concentrated.

"Cultivation of *gong* should begin with *wuji*; yin and yang, and opening and closing, should be pursued conscientiously." Each exercise should begin with the *wuji* commencing posture. In the rest of the text, the term "*wuji* commencing posture" will be used without further explanation to refer to the posture described above. (Figure 5.1)

FIGURE 5.1

2. Descending qi to wash the internal organs

Movement 1: Start with the *wuji* commencing posture. Slowly raise both hands along the sides of the body to a position above the head. At this point, both arms are naturally straight with the two palms facing each other. Inhale while raising the hands. (Figures 5.2, 5.3)

FIGURE 5.2

FIGURE 5.3

Movement 2: The hands come together so that the palms face downward and the fingers point to each other. The hands travel downward, first slowly passing the face, chest, and abdomen, and then finally returning to their original positions. Exhale while lowering the hands. Do further repetitions of the exercise. (Figures 5.4, 5.5)

FIGURE 5.4   FIGURE 5.5

Intent: The intent leads the natural *qi* to integrate with one's own internal *qi* and flow downward, like rain or dew, washing, from exterior to interior, the *baihai* (bones of the body), the limbs, and the five Zang-organs and the six Fu-organs. The intent may stay for a short while at sites of ailment and then lead the pathogenic *qi* out through the *yongquan* point on the sole. While lowering *qi*, the tip of the tongue should be lowered to the floor of the mouth, the mouth should be slightly open, and the exhalation should be slow and even. While exhaling, the intent should be to discharge turbid and abnormal *qi* inside the Lungs out through the mouth.

Point for concentration: The *yongquan*, on the sole, in the depression between the anterior third and posterior two-thirds of the sole.

Efficacy: Wash the five Zang-organs and the six Fu-organs, replace turbid *qi* with clear *qi*, dredge and activate the meridians, conserve essence, and reinforce prenatal (*yuan*) *qi*. Also, the exercise is especially effective against excess in the upper parts and deficiency in the lower parts, high blood pressure, dizziness, headache, excess of Liver *qi*, and insomnia, among others. After completing the exercise, the brain should feel refreshed, the spirit in harmony, and the vision clearer.

Advice: When practicing *neigong*, this exercise should be the first one to practice.

B. GATHERING QI
1. Gathering qi from nature

Movement 1: Start with the *wuji* commencing posture. Take a step forward with the left foot and raise both hands slowly to the front, where the hands should be shoulder-width apart and the arms naturally straight. Shift the center of gravity from the right foot to the left, focus sight on an eye-level object in the distance, and exhale. (Figures 5.6, 5.7)

FIGURE 5.6   FIGURE 5.7

Movement 2: Change both hands into loose fists and draw them back to a location right in front of the middle *dantian* while shifting the center of gravity back to the right foot from the left. Return the eyesight from far to near and finally view the middle *dantian* internally. Inhale while doing the movement. Do further repetitions of the exercise with a pause before each repetition. Then do the same exercise from the right side. (Figures 5.8, 5.9a, b)

FIGURE 5.8

FIGURE 5.9A

FIGURE 5.9B

Intent: The intent, breath, eyes, and movements should be coordinated with each other. Imagine that the essence of nature's *qi* is gathered and stored in the middle *dantian* like a steady stream through gathering with the hands, absorbing through the eyes, and breathing.

Point for concentration: The middle *dantian.*

Efficacy: Cultivate and replenish the *qi* of the *dantian.* Inhale clear *qi* and exhale turbid *qi* through deep breath during the exercise, thus improving the functions of the Lung. The metabolism in the Lung can be enhanced to restore blood oxygen levels and increase the blood's oxygen-carrying capacity. The Lung governs *qi* in the entire body and it is the provider to all meridians and collaterals, so the exercise promotes the circulation of *qi* and blood throughout the body.

Advice: The exercise for gathering *qi* from nature is suitable for all practitioners and can be practiced every season of the year. In fact, it is a compulsory part of every *neigong* session.

In the exercise of gathering *qi* from nature, breathing is done with both the mouth and the nose, which also means that the postnatal breathing method is employed. However, the nose should be used for inhalation and the mouth for exhalation, which is different from normal breathing. The inhalation and exhalation should be even, deep, and long.

If a period of diligent *neigong* practice does not seem to bring the desired result, more time should be dedicated to practicing the gathering *qi* exercise. Gathering *qi* is like refueling a car.

2. Gathering yang qi from heaven

Movement 1: Start with the *wuji* commencing posture. Slowly raise both hands along the sides of the body to a position above the head. At this point, both arms are naturally straight with the two palms facing each other. Look to the sky. Inhale while raising the hands. (Figures 5.10, 5.11)

FIGURE 5.10

FIGURE 5.11

Movement 2: Change both hands into loose fists and turn the heart of the fist (palmar side) of each hand to face inwards. Lower the two fists to the level of the upper chest. Then change both fists into palms that face downwards with the fingers of each hand pointing to each other. Lower the eyelids and look inwards to the middle *dantian*. Hold the breath. (Figures 5.12, 5.13)

FIGURE 5.12

FIGURE 5.13

Movement 3: With both palms, press slowly down to the position of the middle *dantian* and sink the body along with the palms, finally returning to the original posture. Exhale at the same time. Look, think, and listen to the middle *dantian* while doing the above movements. Do further repetitions of the exercise with a pause before each repetition. (Figures 5.14, 5.15)

FIGURE 5.14   FIGURE 5.15

Intent: Imagine that the gathered yang *qi* of the heaven enters the upper *dantian* through the top of the head and then descends to flow into the middle *dantian* like a steady stream. The intent and the hands should be coordinated with each other to gather *qi* with the downward movement of the hands.

Point for concentration: The middle *dantian*.

Efficacy: Employing the method of "three *xing* combine into one" when practicing this exercise can enable spirit to transform into substance and vice versa. The exercise also enables replenishment of yang *qi*, using the gathered yang *qi* to replenish yin *qi*, adjusting yin and yang to keep them in balance, and enriching the internal *qi* of the *dantian*.

Advice: Gathering yang *qi* of the heaven, or yin *qi* of the earth, should be done in accordance with the changes in yin and yang that happen during the different times of day and during the different seasons. Additionally, one's own status of yin *qi* and yang *qi* and balance should be emphasized in the practice. Specifically, those who have deficiency of yang *qi* should increase the time they spend practicing gathering yang *qi* of the heaven, while those who have deficiency of yin *qi* should increase the time they spend practicing gathering yin *qi*. The exercise of gathering natural *qi* is suitable for everyone.

3. Gathering yin qi from the earth

Movement 1: Start with the *wuji* commencing posture. Bend down at the waist and lower both hands to the inner sides of the feet along the inner sides of the legs. (Figures 5.16, 5.17)

FIGURE 5.16   FIGURE 5.17

Movement 2: Make loose fists and raise the fists along the insides of the legs to the position of the crotch while straightening the body. Move both fists, passing by the hips, to the site of the *mingmen* at the lower back. Inhale during the movement. (Figures 5.18, 5.19)

FIGURE 5.18   FIGURE 5.19

Movement 3: After pausing for a while, lower the eyelids and look inwards at the middle *dantian*. Unclench the fists into open hands with the palms facing downwards and move the hands to the site of the middle *dantian* via the sides of the waist. At the same time exhale and slightly lower the body. Repeat the same procedure and always pause before repeating. (Figure 5.20)

FIGURE 5.20

Intent: While raising both hands along the legs, imagine that the gathered yin *qi* of the earth flows from the *yongquan* points via the medial sides of the legs first to the *huiyin*, then to the *weilü* and the *mingmen*, and finally to the middle *dantian*, like a steady stream.

Point for concentration: The middle *dantian*.

Efficacy: The exercise enables use of the gathered yin *qi* to replenish yang *qi*, to adjust yin and yang to keep them balanced in the body, to increase sperm production, to replenish the Kidney *qi*, and transform the essence into *qi*. The gathered natural *qi*, yang *qi* of the heaven, and yin *qi* of the earth all accumulate at the middle *dantian*. Accumulating more and more *qi* lays a foundation for the next step of moving *qi* through the meridians and collaterals.

Advice: While raising the hands, the intent and the movements should be in cooperation. Furthermore, the *huiyin* and the anus should be pulled up (i.e., "lift" the pelvic floor) in coordination with the movement.

C. STANDING POST (ZHAN ZHUANG) EXERCISES

1. Lower dantian standing post

Movements: Start with the *wuji* commencing posture. Position both hands at the lower abdomen with the hands open, the palms facing upwards, the fingers pointing to each other, and a distance of about 20cm between the hands. Flatten the lower back, tuck in the buttocks, and assume a very slightly seated position. At the same time, tuck in the *weilü* (coccyx) and pull up the anus and the *huiyin*. Inhale naturally. (Figure 5.21)

FIGURE 5.21

Intent 1: Gently close the eyes and look inwards, close the ears and listen inwards, and concentrate on the lower *dantian*.

Intent 2: Concentrate on the *huiyin* and adopt the mind/intent breathing method to first inhale and then exhale. Inhale from the *huiyin* 10cm inward and lift up the anus at the same time, and then exhale from the lower *dantian* to the *yongquan* via the two legs. A beginner may freely choose the routes through which the exhaled air goes to the *yongquan* points on the two soles, as long as the mind/intent reaches the *yongquan*. Move the center of gravity and both hands up and down slowly following the inhalation and exhalation of the mind/intent. One inhalation and one exhalation is one complete round. Repetitions should be made.

Intent 3: Change into natural breath and concentrate on the *huiyin*. Motion or stillness should no longer be intentional—just concentrate on the *huiyin* in a state of "three *xing* combine into one" for the rest of the exercise.

Point for concentration: The lower *dantian*, a region inwards from the *huiyin*, corresponding to the prostate (male) or the mouth of the uterus (female).

Efficacy: Concentration on the lower *dantian* nourishes and generates essence, and transforms it into *qi*. Enhanced function of the Kidney benefits the relations between the Heart and the Kidney, promotes the harmony between the Heart and the Kidney and the complementary relations between water and fire, and lays the foundation for overall harmonization of the functions of the organs. Additionally, making the linkage between the *du* and *ren* meridians enables internal *qi* to circulate in the big heavenly circuit (*da zhou tian*) or small heavenly circuit (*xiao zhou tian*).

To those who have deficiency of essence or excessive loss of blood through menstruation, the exercise has the ability to increase the production of essence and blood, and the ability to refine the adjustment of essence and menstrual blood in the body. The exercise compensates the deficiencies and has a good healing effect.

Advice: After a period of practicing concentration on the lower *dantian*, male practitioners may get an erection. This is a sign that the practitioner has sufficient essence. The advice then is to move on to the next step and concentrate on the *mingmen* or the middle *dantian* in order to transform essence into *qi*.

2. Middle dantian standing post

Movements: Start with the *wuji* commencing posture. Raise both hands to a position about 33cm in front of the navel with the hands open, the palms facing inwards, and the fingers pointing to each other. The arms, back, and crotch should be rounded—a reason why the posture is also called the "three circle post" (*san yuan zhuang*). Breathe naturally. (Figure 5.22)

Figure 5.22

Intent 1: Using the "three *xing* combine into one" method, concentrate on the middle *dantian*. Imagine that the posture is round and *qi* is round.

Intent 2: Induce orifice breathing by coordinating the mind/intent with the breathing. First, slowly pull the navel in (orifice inhalation) while inhaling as deeply as possible until the navel seems to touch the *mingmen*. Then exhale and relax the abdomen outwards while imagining the internal *qi* of the *dantian* expanding forwards from the *mingmen* towards the navel. The *dantian* will feel filled up with *qi*. When the abdomen has expanded as far as it will go, start the next round of inhalation and exhalation. Move the body slightly forward and backward with the breathing movement.

Intent 3: Change into natural breath. Pay no attention to the possible movements at the *dantian*. If there is movement, just let it happen. If there is no movement, concentrate on the middle *dantian* in the state of "three *xing* combine into one." Practice the middle *dantian* standing post exercise for 20 minutes or more each time.

Point for concentration: The middle *dantian*.

Efficacy: Concentration on the middle *dantian* nourishes and increases *qi* and transforms *qi* into spirit. Along with the progress made in cultivation, *qi* will gradually build up in the *dantian* and eventually become sufficient. The sufficient internal *qi* promotes the circulation of *qi* in the organs, meridians and collaterals, and blood vessels.

Furthermore, the exercise improves practitioners' instinct of health protection and disease prevention. *Qi* is closely related with blood, and if *qi* is deficient, blood cannot remain unaffected. Deficiency of blood will weaken the resistance to diseases. As a result, functions of various organs will be impaired and diseases caused.

In Qigong practice, concentration on the middle *dantian* can restore prenatal *qi*, improve resistance to diseases (replenishing, nourishing, and strengthening *qi*), make up the deficiency of *qi* and blood, promote the circulation of *qi* and blood, and adjust and improve the functions of various organs to promote recovery. Moreover, the abdominal breathing strengthens the peristalsis of the stomach and intestines, which improves digestion, and adjusts *qi* and blood as well as dredges and activates the meridians.

Advice: After exercising for a period of time, a practitioner will feel that "the two Kidneys are as hot as boiled water and the *dantian* is like a burning fire," which indicates harmony between the Heart and the Kidney, and coordination of water and fire. The practitioner will witness internal images of *qi* rising and running through the meridians and yang *qi* ascending.

Concentration on the middle *dantian* is advised for those who have severe *qi* deficiency of the Spleen, disharmony between the Spleen and the Stomach, digestion system disorders, weak physique, or deficiency of internal *qi*.

3. Upper dantian standing post

Movements: Start with the *wuji* commencing posture. Raise both hands to the eye level with the hands open, palms facing inwards and about 30cm from the face, and the fingers pointing to each other. Round the arms, the back, and the crotch. Breathe naturally. (Figure 5.23)

FIGURE 5.23

Intent 1: Gaze at an eye-level object in the distance. After gazing for a moment, take the sight back slowly and use the intent to lead the hands backwards to collect *qi*. Look inwards to the upper *dantian*. Then concentrate calmly and tranquilly on the upper *dantian* in the state of "three *xing* combine into one."

Intent 2: Use the intent to guide the *qi* of the spirit to extend and return. At the same time, move the hands forwards and backwards and use them to drive the body slightly forwards and backwards as well. When returning the *qi*, inhale slightly to the upper *dantian*; when extending the *qi*, exhale. Do further repetitions of the cycle.

Intent 3: After finishing the previous step, change into natural breath. Concentrate calmly and tranquilly on the upper *dantian* in the state of "three *xing* combine into one." Do not devote your mind to the upper *dantian*. Instead, try to enter into a state where the intent seems to exist and does not seem to exist, and you seem to concentrate and do not seem to concentrate. When closing the exercise, use the intent to lead the spirit and *qi* to sink to the middle *dantian*, and end the exercise shortly after transforming the spirit into void.

Point for concentration: The upper *dantian*.

Efficacy: Concentration on the upper *dantian* nourishes the spirit and transforms it into void.

Advice: Beginners should practice step by step. The exercise of concentrating on the upper *dantian* can be practiced when one's *neigong* has reached a certain level. If the exercise is done too early or if the main points of the exercise are not followed, symptoms such as disorder in the *qi* mechanism or dizziness and/or fullness of the head may appear. Therefore, concentration on the upper *dantian* should be practiced under the guidance of a qualified teacher.

The upper *dantian* is the site where all yang assemble. Practitioners suffering from a downward trend of *qi* due to its deficiency, causing wind and cold of the head, insufficient blood supply in the head, or low blood pressure, are suitable for the exercise of concentrating on the upper *dantian*. Those with excessive fire due to yin deficiency, flaming up of Heart fire, hyperactive Liver yang ascending abnormally, or high blood pressure are advised not to practice concentrating on the upper *dantian* in order to avoid aggravating the diseases.

D. REGULATING AND BALANCING YIN AND YANG

1. Inflating two poles with qi

Movement 1: Stand in the *wuji* commencing posture with the feet shoulder-width apart. Raise both hands and bring them in front of the abdomen with the arms curved. Keep the two hands about 10cm apart with the hands open and the *laogong* points at the center of each hand facing each other. Lower the eyelids and concentrate on the *laogong* for a while. When there is a feeling of *qi* in the hands, start to move. Part the hands slowly to the sides, like drawing a rubber band, to a width of one meter or so. At this point the two arms are shaped like a bow. Inhale while moving the hands apart. (Figures 5.24, 5.25)

FIGURE 5.24   FIGURE 5.25

Movement 2: Move the hands closer and stop when they have reached their original positions. Exhale while doing the movement. Do further repetitions of the exercise.

Intent: Concentrate the intent and *qi* between the two *laogong*. When parting the hands, the intent and *qi* open. When closing the two hands, the intent and *qi* close. Meanwhile, concentrate on the breath at the *laogong*, look inwards at the breath at the *laogong*, and listen inwards to the breath at the *laogong*. There the inhalation is soft and continuous and the exhalation is faint.

Point for concentration: The *laogong*, at the center of the palm.

Efficacy: Various changes of *qi* between the two *laogong* and the two palms can be sensed. Parting the hands is like drawing a rubber band, and there is a feeling of pressure between the hands when closing them—precisely the attracting and repelling forces in a magnetic field. If one's *gongfu* has reached a certain level, he can feel bulging and vibration at the *laogong* when the internal *qi* rushes there.

Advice: Use the hands to lead the opening and closing of the chest and the abdomen, and the opening and closing of the internal *qi* in the *dantian*.

2. Coordinating the water and the fire

Movements: Stand in the *wuji* commencing posture with the feet shoulder-width apart. Relax the waist and the lower back, tuck the buttocks in, sink the shoulders, and empty the chest. Place the hands on the back at the site of the *mingmen* with the palms inwards and the fingers pointing to each other. (Figures 5.26, 5.27)

FIGURE 5.26   FIGURE 5.27

Breath: Inhale through nose; exhale through mouth.

Intent: Imagine using the fire of the heart spirit (*xin shen*) to burn the firewood in the *mingmen* to boil the water in the Kidney. On exhalation, imagine blowing on the fire at the *mingmen* to make the fire stronger.

After long-term practice, and with good enough *neigong*, one may feel a sensation of heat arise at the *mingmen*. As one's *neigong* improves, the feeling will expand to the entire area of the *dantian*. This signifies reaching a new stage in one's cultivation practice, which in *neigong* terms is described as "the two Kidneys are as hot as boiled water and the *dantian* is like a burning fire."

Point for concentration: The *mingmen*.

Efficacy: As adding firewood strengthens fire, so concentration on the *mingmen* and the two Kidneys will strengthen the waist, improve the Kidneys, and promote the process of transforming essence into *qi*.

Advice: In Taoist Qigong and Chinese traditional medicine, it is believed that the relationship between the Heart and the Kidneys is primarily that of mutual assistance of yin and yang (or water and fire) and secondly that of mutual dependence between vital essence and spirit. The Heart, located in the Upper Jiao, has a dynamic nature and gives priority to yang (fire), whereas the Kidneys, located in the Lower Jiao, have a stable nature (to store essence) and give priority to yin (water).

When Heart yang descends, it makes Kidney yin warm. When Kidney yin ascends, it nourishes Heart yang. The upper and the lower meet, linking motion and stability, which makes the two opposites identical and keeps the body in a relative balance all the time. This phenomenon is also called "coordination of water and fire" and "coordination of the Heart and the Kidneys."

If yang *qi* is insufficient and Kidney water does not cooperate, the water *qi* will invade upwards and palpitation of the Heart will be caused by "water *qi* attacking the Heart." If Kidney water is insufficient and unable to ascend and harmonize Heart fire, Heart fire will be excessive and it will cause diseases of "disharmony between the Heart and the Kidneys," including insomnia, amnesia, tinnitus, tiredness, weakness of the legs, excessive dreaming, and involuntary seminal emissions.

The Heart governs the storage of spirit and the Kidneys govern the storage of essence. Spirit and essence oppose each other and unite with each other. Essence serves as the material foundation of spirit, whereas the spirit acts as the external appearance of essence. The congenital essence serves as the material prerequisite to spirit, whereas the acquired essence replenishes spirit. The sufficiency of essence and *qi* empowers spirit to act, whereas the exuberance of spirit enables the essence to regenerate. Consequently, when talking about a health situation, the terms essence and spirit are commonly used.

3. Duckweed floating in the water

Movement 1: Stand in the *wuji* commencing posture with the feet shoulder-width apart. Lower the two arms naturally, placing the hands about 15cm away from the hips with the hands open, palms facing downward, and the fingers pointing forward. Stand still and concentrate on the *laogong* using the "three *xing* combine into one" method.

After concentrating for a while, change into a moving exercise. Press down slowly with the left hand while shifting the center of gravity to the left foot. Simultaneously raise the right hand gently to the chest level. (Figures 5.28, 5.29)

FIGURE 5.28   FIGURE 5.29

Movement 2: Press down slowly with the right hand while shifting the center of gravity to the right foot from the left. Simultaneously raise the left hand gently to the chest level. Do further repetitions of the exercise. (Figure 5.30)

FIGURE 5.30

Intent: Concentrate on the *laogong* and the *yongquan*. When intent arrives, *qi* arrives, and the center of gravity should arrive as well. In this exercise, the body is like a balance scale, coordinating the internal and the external and regulating the five balance systems of the human body.

Point for concentration: The *laogong* and the *yongquan*.

Efficacy: The balance systems will be adjusted, improved, and strengthened via coordinating the intent and movements like a pair of balances.

Advice: When practicing this exercise, it is essential to make sure that, when intent arrives, both *qi* and the center of gravity arrive. The internal should integrate with the external.

E. GREAT POWER EXERCISES

1. Opening and closing

Movement 1: Stand in the *wuji* commencing posture with the feet a bit wider than shoulder-width apart. Cross the arms in front of the body and, passing in front of the abdomen and the chest, raise them slowly to a position above the head. Part the crossed arms to their respective sides until they naturally straighten at a level slightly higher than the shoulders. Open the chest and the abdomen with the opening movement of the arms and slightly raise the body and the center of gravity. Inhale while doing this movement. (Figures 5.31, 5.32)

FIGURE 5.31   FIGURE 5.32

Movement 2: Clench the fingers into empty fists, like grabbing something. Lower the hands slowly, finally crossing the wrists in front of the abdomen with the hearts of the fists facing inward. Bend the knees, sink the body, and close the chest and the abdomen with the closing movement of the arms. Exhale while doing this movement. Do further repetitions of the exercise. (Figures 5.33, 5.34)

FIGURE 5.33   FIGURE 5.34

Intent: While opening the chest and the abdomen, imagine that the *dantian qi* runs upwards from the *mingmen* along the spine, goes through the shoulders and elbows, and reaches the hands. Inhale at the same time. Having inhaled as deeply as possible, clench the fingers and lead the chest and the abdomen to close, and exhale in coordination with the closing. At the same time, while imagining grabbing *qi* and gathering and restoring it to the middle *dantian*, gradually bulge out the abdominal area near the navel to get a rich and full feeling to the *dantian*, multiplying your vigor.

Point for concentration: The middle *dantian*.

Efficacy: The opening and closing movements induce the opening and closing of *qi*, which has the effects of strengthening *qi*, enhancing physical strength, enriching the *dantian*, and accumulating energy.

Advice: When the movement is to open, the thought of opening should be held in mind. When any part of the body opens, there is no part that does not open. *Qi* expanding to the entire body should be imagined. Conversely, when the movement is to close, the thought of closing should be held in mind. When any part of the body closes, there is no part that does not close. All *qi* and power in the entire body should gradually gather to the *dantian*.

2. Dragon playing in the water

Movement 1: Start with the *wuji* commencing posture. Take one step forward with the right foot, leaving the center of gravity on the left foot. The left leg is bent. Put both hands on the site of the *mingmen*. With the hands open and the palms facing upward, move the hands to the front of the abdomen via the hips. At this point, the little fingers of the hands should touch each other. Continue by stretching both arms forward until they become naturally straight at a level slightly lower than the shoulders. At the same time, move the body forward and shift the weight from the left foot to the right foot following the movement of the hands. Exhale while doing this movement. (Figures 5.35, 5.36)

FIGURE 5.35   FIGURE 5.36

Movement 2: Relax and lower both hands naturally. Move the hands back to the site of the *mingmen* via the hips while moving the body backward and shifting the center of gravity back to the left foot to restore the original posture. Inhale while doing this movement. Do further repetitions of the exercise. (Figures 5.37, 5.38)

FIGURE 5.37   FIGURE 5.38

Intent: While moving the hands to the front of the abdomen and stretching the arms forward, imagine that the internal *qi* moves upward from the *mingmen* along the spine and runs to the fingertips via the shoulders, elbows, and hands.

Point for concentration: The *laogong*.

Efficacy: Enhances the ability to use the internal *qi* of the *dantian* for driving *qi* to run through the nine sections and makes *qi* arrive when intent arrives and force arrive when *qi* arrives.

Advice: When doing the exercise, the knee of the front leg should not pass the tips of the toes and the body should be kept centered and upright.

3. Spiral punch

Movement 1: Start with the *santi* standing post posture: take a step forward with the right foot, lower the center of gravity to the left foot, bend the left knee, tuck in the abdomen, and tuck in the buttocks. Raise the right hand to shoulder level with the palm facing outward, keeping the hand aligned with the foot, the elbow aligned with the knee, and the shoulder aligned with the hip. Put the left hand on the side of the left hip with the palm facing downward, sink the shoulder, and drop the elbow. Let *qi* sink to the *dantian*. In quiescence, use the internal sight to watch the right *laogong*.

After standing still for a while, change into a moving exercise. Withdraw the right hand to the side of the right hip and change the open hand into a fist with the heart of the fist facing upward. At the same time, change the left hand into a fist with the heart of the fist facing upward, turn the waist and the spine, and spirally thrust the left fist forward to an end position where the fist is at the heart level with the heart of the fist facing downward and the arm is naturally straight. Focus your eyes on the thrusting fist and keep the weight on the left foot. (Figures 5.39, 5.40)

FIGURE 5.39   FIGURE 5.40

Movement 2: Turn from the waist and thrust the right fist spirally forward from the side of the hip to an end position where the arm is naturally straight and the fist is at the heart level with the heart of the fist facing downward. Watch the thrusting fist and shift the center of gravity from the left foot to the right foot, changing into a bow step with the right knee bent and pressing down with the left foot. Breathe naturally. Do further repetitions of the exercise and after that do the exercise with the other foot in front. (Figure 5.41)

FIGURE 5.41

Intent: While thrusting the fist, use intent to lead *qi* to run out of the middle *dantian* to the fist, passing through the *mingmen*, back, shoulder, and elbow.

Point for concentration: The middle *dantian* and *laogong*.

Efficacy: When intent arrives, *qi* arrives, and when *qi* arrives, physical force arrives automatically. The body and *qi* move spirally, and energy (*jin*) lands on one point and penetrates the bones.

A practitioner who has reached the stage of external *dan gong* may return to this exercise for deeper experience. Whenever he thrusts his fist forward, he may feel that a *qi* ball moves together with the fist, and when he withdraws the fist and relaxes, the *qi* ball follows the fist and returns to the *dantian*. If his *gongfu* is of high standard, the intent and *qi* reach far and they will be well controlled regardless of the distance.

Advice: At first, movements should be slow, to satisfy the requirement of "when intent arrives, *qi* and force arrive." When the exercise is perfectly executed, a higher speed of movement can be used.

F. CLOSING EXERCISES

1. Closing movements for each exercise

Movement 1: At the end of each *neigong* exercise, return to a shoulder-width standing posture. Raise both hands slowly along the sides of the body to a position above the head with the arms naturally straight, the palms facing each other, and the hands shoulder-width apart. Inhale while raising the hands. (Figures 5.42, 5.43)

FIGURE 5.42

FIGURE 5.43

Movement 2: Bring the hands closer together so that the fingers point to each other and the palms face downward. Lower the hands to the level of the middle *dantian* on the abdomen via the face and the chest. At the same time, lower the center of gravity following the movement of the hands, and return to the *wuji* posture. Exhale while lowering the hands. (Figures 5.44–5.46)

FIGURE 5.44

FIGURE 5.45

FIGURE 5.46

Intent: Guided by the movements, use the intent to guide *qi* collected during the exercise to descend and accumulate at the middle *dantian*.

Point for concentration: The middle *dantian*.

Efficacy: The middle *dantian* works like a water reservoir, only storing, not leaking. The more *qi* that is accumulated, the more there will be.

Advice: This closing exercise should be done at the end of each *neigong* exercise.

2. Five kinds of qi return to the origin

Movements: Start with the *wuji* commencing posture. Put the right palm on the navel and put the left palm on the back of the right hand. Move the overlapped hands in counterclockwise circles (to the left, up, right, down, and so on) slowly around the navel 36 times. The circumference of the circles should gradually increase from small to large. (Figure 5.47a)

Exchange the positions of the hands and slowly make 24 clockwise circles from large to small with a gradually decreasing circumference. Breathe naturally. (Figure 5.47b)

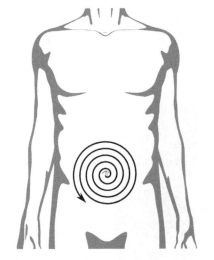 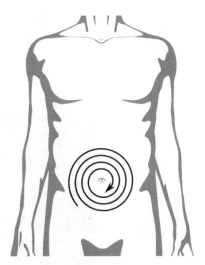

FIGURE 5.47A COUNTERCLOCKWISE
MOVEMENT FOR MALES

FIGURE 5.47B CLOCKWISE
MOVEMENT FOR MALES

Intent: Concentrate tranquilly on the middle *dantian* in the state of "three *xing* combine into one" for a while and imagine at the same time that the *qi* at the *laogong* points of the hands connects with the internal *qi* at the *dantian*. With the navel as the center, integrate the sight with intent and the internal with the external to rotate *qi* counterclockwise in circles of increasing circumference. This movement is called "disperse *qi* with counterclockwise (*ni*) rotation."

After that, lead *qi* with the sight and intent to rotate clockwise in circles of decreasing circumference. Collect *qi* scattered in the body and restore it to the middle *dantian*. This movement is called "return *qi* with clockwise (*shun*) rotation."

The above description of the movements is for male practitioners. The directions and the hand placement is the opposite for female practitioners: the 36 circles of increasing circumference are done clockwise with the left hand placed under the right hand, and the 24 circles of decreasing circumference are done counterclockwise with the right hand under the left hand. (Figures 5.48a, b)

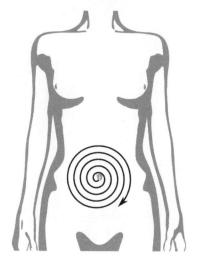 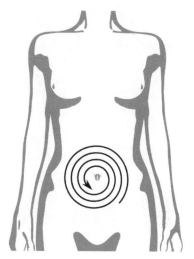

FIGURE 5.48A CLOCKWISE MOVEMENT FOR FEMALES

FIGURE 5.48B COUNTERCLOCKWISE MOVEMENT FOR FEMALES

Point for concentration: The middle *dantian*.

Efficacy: The exercise is designed to first disperse the internal *qi* collected during the exercise in order to avoid the stasis of *qi*, and then gather the dispersed *qi* along with the essential *qi* of the five Zang-organs distributed throughout the body during the exercise and restore them to the middle *dantian*, merging them into one.

Advice: Concentrate on the rotation of *qi* in the *dantian*, and look and listen inwards to the rotation of *qi* in the *dantian*. The internal *qi* and the hands should rotate around the *dantian*, dispersing *qi* circle by circle or gathering *qi* circle by circle.

CHAPTER VI

The Thirteen Postures of Taijiquan

A. EXERCISES OF THE EIGHT TECHNIQUES OF TAIJIQUAN

1. Warding-off energy

While practicing push-hands, the opening and closing and storing and releasing movements of the body and the limbs, along with the surging and withdrawing movements of the internal *qi*, produce a kind of force that supports an elastic energy, called warding-off (*peng*) energy (*jin*), in all directions. The elastic energy, or "elastic force" in the terminology of mechanics, is quite common in daily life. For example, if you study how a spring works, you might notice the following: the larger the elastic deformation (e.g., compressing or stretching a spring from its resting form) of an object is, the more powerful its elastic force will be; the smaller the elastic deformation is, the less powerful the elastic force will be; and if the elastic deformation disappears, the elastic force will disappear as well. The elastic deformation, however, is within certain limits, and the direction of the elastic force always depends on how the deformed object restores to its original shape.

In accordance with the above, warding-off energy is also called "spring energy" in Taijiquan terminology. The theoretical sayings of Taijiquan are in line with the principle of elastic force as well; for example: "Follow the opponent's bending or stretching," "Seek for the straight in the curved," "Accumulate energy like drawing a bow and emit energy like shooting an arrow," and "Equipped with five bows in the body, maintain force in all directions."

Therefore, while exercising Taiji push-hands or fighting techniques, if a practitioner can really internalize the forms and functions of a spring or a bow in order to keep his arms curved all the time and to make his entire body elastic and work like a spring or a bow, then he will be able to attack back with the spring energy whenever the opponent attacks.

When a practitioner's internal power has developed so well that his *dantian* is full of *qi*, his body will be like a spheroid filled with internal *qi* which exists in the skin and muscles, and condenses into the marrow. The richer the internal *qi* is, the more powerful the spring energy is able to be, and the better the quality of warding-off energy is as well. Therefore, warding-off energy is also considered a condensed display of Taijiquan *gongfu*.

Warding-off energy is the major energy among the eight techniques of Taiji and also the general energy among the thirteen postures of Taiji. The eight techniques of Taiji are derived from variations of warding-off energy at different positions and in different directions; for example: warding-off energy is generated when a practitioner rotates upward to spring back after being pressed by the opponent; rolling-back (*lü*) energy is generated when the practitioner rotates leftward or rightward to spring back after being pressed; pressing (*ji*) energy is generated when the practitioner rotates forward to spring back after being pressed; and pushing (*an*) energy is generated when a practitioner rotates downward to spring back after being pressed.

Warding-off energy exists in the other seven kinds of energy. Without the support of warding off energy, a practitioner will be weak in Taiji push-hands, and he may make the mistakes of separating with the opponent or yielding while leading and trying to divert the intruding energy, withstanding or resisting while trying to neutralize and pitch the opponent out, or disintegrating and slacking while relaxing.

The methods of applying warding-off energy include: warding off with the arms, warding off with the chest, warding off with the abdomen, warding off with the back, warding off with the buttocks, and warding off with the legs.

The technical characteristics of warding-off energy include that it is emitted from the inside to the outside in a state where intent (*yi*), *qi*, and movements combine into one, acting outwardly as warding-off movements, internally as warding off energy, and, applied to the opponent, as warding-off techniques.

Solo exercise

Movements: Assume a *wuji* commencing posture. Step out with the right foot. Lift both hands slowly up to a position a little higher than the shoulders with the two hands facing downward, the fingers of each hand kept together in a natural way, and the two arms and the body (chest) forming a circle. At the same time, bend the knees and lower the center of gravity. Make a step forward with the left foot and make a movement of warding off again. Advance forward by making further repetitions. (Figures 6.1–6.3)

FIGURE 6.1   FIGURE 6.2

FIGURE 6.3

Partner exercise

Movements: Each partner makes a step with the right foot. *B* (in black) bends the right knee, presses down with the left foot, and at the same time pushes *A* (in white) on the chest with both hands. *A* raises both arms and uses warding-off energy to lift *B*'s arms and hands up, thus rendering *B*'s efforts futile. *A* and *B* complete the same exercise with their roles exchanged and do further repetitions of the exercise. (Figures 6.4, 6.5)

FIGURE 6.4

FIGURE 6.5

Efficacy: The exercise is helpful for developing the qualities of warding-off energy: making intent round, *qi* round, and external appearance round, and developing a quality where an external force being applied from the outside will cause the warding-off energy to spring out from the inside.

Advice: While doing the warding-off movements, note that they should be done from the inside to the outside and an inter-supporting mechanism between the upper and lower, right and left, and back and front should be formed in order to meet the requirement of providing support in all directions. In the partner exercise, the practitioners should not separate from each other or withstand or block each other.

2. Rolling-back energy

Rolling-back (*lü*) energy is one of the forms of neutralizing energy. While applying rolling-back energy, a practitioner should "give up himself and follow the opponent; gain victory by following the opponent." In Taiji push-hands, the more powerful the intruding energy is, the more powerful the inertia will be. Therefore, we should take advantage of the opponent's inertia and use rolling-back energy to make the opponent lean forward and fail to keep his centered and upright state. The opponent may be thrown to the ground if rolling-back energy is skillfully applied.

Thinking of the intruding energy as a flood, if you try to enclose and block up the flood, it will inevitably burst through the banks. However, if you divert the flood away from its original course to your left or right side, you will not be lashed by the flood. At the same time, you can, according to the fundamentals of inertia and resultant force, add your own energy to the opponent's body in the same direction as the diversion so that the opponent's center of gravity will be guided to go beyond the centered and upright scope. The opponent will lose balance or fall.

The above is an example of "Give up yourself and follow the opponent, guide the opponent to enter into emptiness, and use energy by borrowing the intruding energy." While using rolling-back energy, warding-off energy is often used in combination with it in order to make "the elbow not touch the ribs" and, also, to protect oneself from being attacked at one's central gate by the opponent, or "inviting a wolf into the house" in other words.

The techniques for applying rolling-back energy include: single-handed rolling back, two-handed rolling back, rolling back with the elbow, rolling back with the chest, rolling back with the abdomen, and rolling back with the legs.

The technical characteristics of rolling-back energy include that, in a state where intent, *qi*, and external movements are merged with each other, it guides the target parts of the opponent's body or limbs backward, to the left and back or to the right and back, acting outwardly as rolling-back movements, internally as rolling-back energy, and, applied to the opponent, as rolling-back techniques.

Solo exercise

Movements: Assume a *wuji* commencing posture. Make a step forward with the right foot, bend the right knee, and shift the center of gravity to the right foot. At the same time, raise both arms to the shoulder level with the two arms naturally straight and both palms facing left. Roll back with both palms and meanwhile turn from the waist and shift the center of gravity gradually to the left foot following the rolling-back movement. Make a step forward with the left foot and exercise the movements of rolling back, with the same main points, on the right side. Move forward by doing further repetitions of the exercise. (Figures 6.6–6.8)

FIGURE 6.6   FIGURE 6.7

FIGURE 6.8

Partner exercise

Movements: *B* steps out with the right foot and pushes with his right palm on *A*'s chest; *A* grasps *B*'s right wrist with the right hand, holds *B*'s right elbow with the left hand, and performs a rolling-back movement to make *B* lose his balance or fall to the ground, taking advantage of the inertia of *B*'s pushing movement. *B* applies rolling back in the same way to *A*. *A* and *B* complete the same exercise with their roles exchanged and do further repetitions of the exercise. (Figures 6.9–6.11)

FIGURE 6.9

FIGURE 6.10

FIGURE 6.11

Efficacy: The exercise enables a practitioner to use rolling-back energy to abandon himself and follow the opponent, to guide the opponent to enter into emptiness, and to use energy by borrowing the opponent's energy as well as to roll back the opponent's tip section to break the opponent's root.

Advice: While using rolling-back energy, warding-off energy should be cooperatively applied. The combined application of the energies can protect the applier from being attacked by the opponent, who may take advantage of the applier's rolling-back energy to get close and attack. When the opponent is being guided to enter into emptiness but has not yet been pitched out or down to the ground, the practitioner should quickly continue to emit energy to pitch the opponent out. The same is stated in Taijiquan theory as "Guide the opponent to enter into emptiness and immediately attack."

3. *Pressing energy*

Pressing (*ji*)—or, literally, squeezing—energy is like a nail being hammered into wood. In push-hands, pressing energy is often applied with the two palms put together forming a sharp wedge to push forward. Pressing energy is called "resultant force" in mechanics. The application of pressing energy, backed by internal power and combined with the techniques of the six harmonies, should merge the intent, *qi*, and external movements into a single point, emit energy at the point, and have the idea of penetrating the target link with the pressing energy.

Taijiquan theory states: "It is necessary for a practitioner being rolled back to know that he should give up himself and follow the opponent in order to seize the opportunity for pressing." It refers to the techniques and tactics of pressing adopted to tackle rolling-back energy.

For instance, when the opponent is applying rolling back to one of your arms, with your center of gravity moving forward and your balance about to be lost, you should abandon yourself and follow the opponent, step forward quickly in line with the opponent's rolling-back movement, and use pressing energy to pitch the opponent out. This example of pressing energy also uses techniques and tactics that are often employed in push-hands. Using pressing energy to beat rolling-back energy, like boating down the river, shows the wonderful quality of following the trend and borrowing force.

The techniques for applying pressing energy include: single-handed pressing, two-handed pressing, pressing with the elbows, and pressing with the knees.

The technical characteristics of pressing energy include that it is emitted forward horizontally in a state where intent, *qi*, and external movements are combined into one, acting outwardly as pressing movements, internally as pressing energy, and, applied to the opponent, as pressing techniques.

Solo exercise

Movements: Adopt a *wuji* commencing posture. Raise the two arms to the front and circle them to the back, each arm on its respective side of the body (similar to a swimming motion), and complete the circle by bringing the two palms together in front of the chest. Keep the fingers of each hand together. Make a step forward with the right foot and push the wedge-like hands forward. At the same time, shift the center of gravity to the right foot and make a bow step. Then, make a step forward with the left foot and exercise the movements on the other side. Advance by doing further repetitions. (Figures 6.12, 6.13)

FIGURE 6.12   FIGURE 6.13

Partner exercise

Movements: *A* makes a step forward with his right foot and *B* does the same. *B* grasps *A*'s two arms and pushes forward forcefully. *A* makes a circle with both arms (similar to the solo exercise above) to neutralize the intruding energy, puts the two palms together to form a wedge, and pushes toward the center of *B*'s body until *B* is pushed out. *A* and *B* complete the same exercise with their roles exchanged and do further repetitions of the exercise. (Figures 6.14–6.16)

FIGURE 6.14

FIGURE 6.15

FIGURE 6.16

Efficacy: Pressing energy functions well in combining the intent with *qi* and external movements, focusing on one point, emitting at one point, and penetrating the opponent.

Advice: When applying pressing energy, the energy should "manifest on the hands, pass through the spine, come from pressing down with the leg, and be controlled by the waist." The practitioner should experience the technical character of "the three external harmonies" and "the three internal harmonies" and carry them out while applying pressing energy. Attention should be paid to the front knee, which is not supposed to pass the toes. Pressing energy should be used after the intruding energy has been neutralized.

4. Pushing energy

An example of pushing (*an*) energy would be when the opponent is pressing forward with all his strength and one utilizes the inertia principle and pushes downward to "guide the opponent to enter into emptiness." At this moment, it is easiest to draw and move the opponent's heels. As the proverb goes: "Push the opponent's tip section to break his root." The opponent may be shocked, feeling that he is suddenly falling down from the air, if a push is skillfully applied.

Pushing energy acts as one's last defensive line. It should be employed at the right time. If pushing energy is applied earlier than it should be, it will be impossible to "guide the opponent to enter into emptiness." However, if a practitioner applies it later than the right time, it will be dangerous for him, like "inviting a wolf into the house," and he could lose his balance from the opponent's intrusion. Therefore, it is vital to choose the correct time for applying pushing energy.

Another method of applying pushing energy is to turn defense into attack, push on a proper part of the opponent, and make him fall after neutralizing his intrusion. Pushing energy can be applied not only in defense but also to attack.

The techniques for applying pushing energy include: pushing with the hands, pushing with the elbows, pushing with the chest, pushing with the abdomen, pushing with the hips, and pushing with the legs.

The technical characteristics of pushing energy include that it is emitted downward, in a state where intent, *qi*, and movements are combined with each other, acting outwardly as pushing movements, internally as pushing energy, and, applied to the opponent, as pushing techniques.

Solo exercise

Movements: Adopt a *wuji* commencing posture. Make a step forward with the right foot, raise both hands to chest level, and push downward until the two arms are straightened naturally. Simultaneously, lower the center of gravity, make the hips seated, keep an arched crotch, and bend the knees following the pushing movement. Make a step forward with the left foot and practice the same exercise. Advance by doing further repetitions of the exercise. (Figures 6.17–6.19)

FIGURE 6.17

FIGURE 6.18

FIGURE 6.19

Partner exercise

Movements: *A* makes a step forward with his right foot and *B* does the same. *B* pushes *A* on the abdomen; *A* pushes *B*'s hands down until *B*'s push enters into emptiness or *B* falls to the ground. *A* and *B* complete the same exercise with their roles exchanged and do further repetitions of the exercise. (Figures 6.20, 6.21)

FIGURE 6.20

FIGURE 6.21

Efficacy: The functions of pushing energy are to "guide the opponent to enter into emptiness" and to "push down the opponent's tip section to break his root."

Advice: While making pushing (down) movements, the intent and *qi* pass down from the *dantian* all the way to the *yongquan* acupoint on the sole. This action links the upper and the lower and keeps the internal and the external in unison to make the root more stable.

While making pushing movements, both hands should push down close to the chest and the abdomen. The movement to push the opponent's hands down looks like brushing the chest and abdomen. Done this way, the pushing technique will be most efficient.

Another point about applying pushing energy is that, while pushing a part of the opponent's body, the practitioner can apply pushing energy effectively only after he has neutralized the attack launched by the opponent.

Illustrations of relations between the body and warding off, rolling back, pressing, and pushing

Warding-off (*peng*) energy refers to the motions moving upward from the horizontal central line. (Figure 6.22)

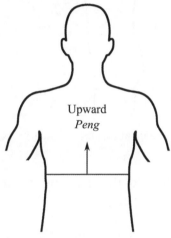

FIGURE 6.22 THE RELATION BETWEEN THE BODY AND WARDING-OFF ENERGY

Rolling-back (*lü*) energy refers to the motions turning around the central axis in the body. (Figure 6.23)

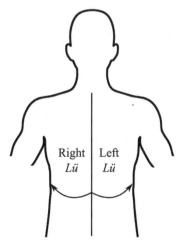

FIGURE 6.23 THE RELATION BETWEEN THE BODY AND ROLLING-BACK ENERGY

Pressing (*ji*) energy refers to the motions moving forward from the center of the body. (Figure 6.24)

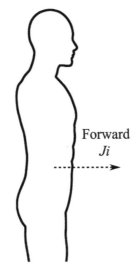

FIGURE 6.24 THE RELATION BETWEEN THE BODY AND PRESSING ENERGY

Pushing (*an*) energy refers to the motions moving downward from the horizontal central line. (Figure 6.25)

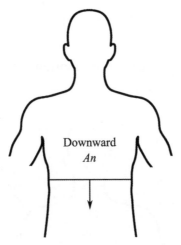

FIGURE 6.25 THE RELATION BETWEEN THE BODY AND PUSHING ENERGY

Rules for circular movement in Taiji

In Taiji push-hands, the body as a whole can be seen as a (Taiji) sphere. The following are the relations between the actions of the Taiji sphere and the energies that the actions generate.

Warding-off energy is created by the Taiji sphere when it rotates upward reacting to an external force. (Figure 6.26)

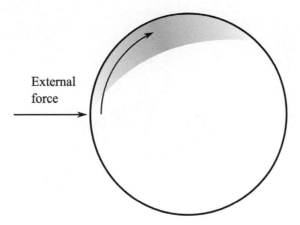

FIGURE 6.26 WARDING-OFF ENERGY IS GENERATED BY THE MOVEMENT OF A SPHERE

Rolling-back energy is created by the Taiji sphere when it rotates backward from the front right or the front left reacting to an external force. (Figure 6.27)

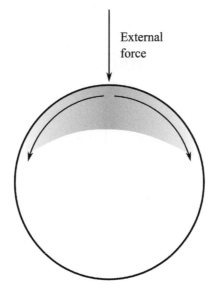

FIGURE 6.27 ROLLING-BACK ENERGY IS GENERATED
BY THE MOVEMENT OF A SPHERE

Pressing energy is created by the Taiji sphere when it springs back and returns to its original shape after being pressed flat by an external force. (Figure 6.28)

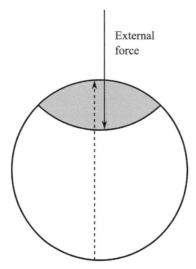

FIGURE 6.28 PRESSING ENERGY IS GENERATED BY THE MOVEMENT OF A SPHERE

Neutralizing energy is created by the yin side of the Taiji sphere when the sphere rotates from the front to the rear reacting to an external force, whereas pressing energy is created by the yang side when it rotates from the rear to the front. (Figure 6.29)

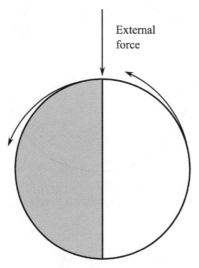

FIGURE 6.29 NEUTRALIZING AND PRESSING ENERGY IS GENERATED BY THE MOVEMENT OF A SPHERE

Pushing energy is created by the Taiji sphere when it rotates downward reacting to an external force. (Figure 6.30)

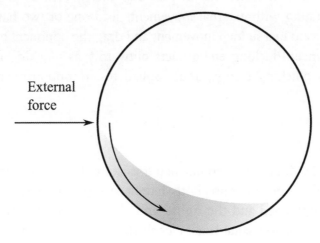

External
force

FIGURE 6.30 PUSHING ENERGY IS GENERATED BY THE MOVEMENT OF A SPHERE

5. Plucking energy

Plucking (*cai*) energy is one of the techniques of seizing and joint-locking (*qinna*). However, the usage of the plucking technique in Taiji push-hands is not quite the same as in seizing and joint-locking. It is listed as one of the eight techniques of Taiji because it has been developed into a unique kind of energy, relying on long-term practice, and it is one of the methods of clinching and dragging the opponent with the hands.

In Taiji push-hands, while an opponent applies a force to a practitioner, the practitioner may suddenly change from light touch to plucking and jerking the opponent with both hands. Because of the high speed, short distance, and accurate landing point of the plucking energy, the opponent may be terrified and feel as if he is falling into a bottomless abyss. The sudden plucking energy functions as a shocking tactic, which may shake the opponent's heels easily. The plucking technique is effective in giving up oneself to follow the opponent and guiding the opponent to enter into emptiness.

Before applying plucking energy, the change of movements should be light and agile or the opponent will be able to sense it and escape. Plucking movements should be sure and firm to clinch and drag the opponent to make him lose his balance or fall. Plucking the opponent's tip section and breaking his root is similar to dragging a wooden stake down.

The techniques for applying plucking energy include: single-handed plucking and two-handed plucking.

The technical characteristics of plucking energy include that the intent and *qi* integrating with external movements lead one or two hands to emit energy backward in a sudden movement and drag the opponent to make him lose his balance. Plucking energy acts outwardly as plucking movements, internally as plucking energy, and, applied to the opponent, as plucking techniques.

Solo exercise

Movements: Adopt a *wuji* commencing posture. Make a big step forward with the right foot and raise both hands to chest level with both arms naturally straightened and the right hand ahead of the left. Withdraw the right foot and, at the same time, clench the fingers and pluck downward and backward to the position beside the right hip. End the exercise with the right leg in front and the left leg at the back and the center of gravity resting on the left leg which is bent.

Step forward with the left foot and do the same movements from the left side. Move forward by doing further repetitions of the above exercise. (Figures 6.31–6.33)

FIGURE 6.31

FIGURE 6.32

FIGURE 6.33

Partner exercise

Movements: *A* makes a step forward with the right foot and *B* does the same. *A* launches an attack upon *B* with his left fist. *B*, with his left hand, grasps *A*'s left wrist. *A* rotates his left hand and grasps *B*'s left wrist, steps further forward with his right foot, and stretches out his right hand and uses it together with his left hand to hold *B*'s left wrist. Then *A* withdraws his two feet and, with his two hands, suddenly plucks *B*'s left wrist to the left, back, and downward until *B* loses his balance or falls. *A* and *B* complete the same exercise with their roles exchanged and do further repetitions of the exercise. (Figures 6.34–6.36)

FIGURE 6.34

FIGURE 6.35

FIGURE 6.36

Efficacy: Plucking energy acts to pluck the opponent's tip section to break his root and to guide the opponent to enter into emptiness.

Advice: While applying plucking energy, it should be combined with warding-off energy to make plucking energy more effective and to avoid the opponent getting a chance of stepping in and launching an attack. Skillful application of plucking energy will shock the opponent's cranial nerve and dislocate his shoulder joint.

The techniques for applying plucking energy also include: plucking the head, plucking the shoulder(s), and plucking the chest.

6. Splitting energy

Generally, splitting (*lie*) energy is applied in coordination with seizing and joint-locking. In fighting, as soon as hands touch, it can be used to control one of the opponent's nine major kinds of joints: shoulders, elbows, hands, hips, knees, feet, neck, spine, or waist.

When the opponent attacks, the practitioner catches a part of the opponent's body or limbs and twists it, wrenches it, and dislocates the concerned joint. As soon as the situation in which the joint is hyperextended has been formed, the practitioner may emit explosive energy simultaneously in two opposite directions, that is to say, using splitting energy.

In push-hands or fighting technique, neutralizing intruding energy for defending or emitting energy for attacking requires the use of force. In mechanics, it is clearly expressed that there are three key elements related with force: strength, direction, and acting point. When two parallel, opposite forces are applied simultaneously, there will be leverage.

The practitioner emits splitting energy in accordance with the lever principle to stop the opponent's attack effectively. In addition, splitting energy is effective for hurting the tendons, for misplacing the bones, for cutting energy or *qi* of a counter-attack, and also for gaining the initiative by striking late. Using splitting energy can also make it impossible for the opponent to bring his force and *gongfu* into normal play.

The techniques for applying splitting energy include: splitting with the hands, splitting with the elbows, splitting with the shoulders, splitting with the chest, splitting with the knees, and hand/foot splitting.

The technical characteristics of splitting energy include that the practitioner catches a part of the opponent and twists it, wrenches it, and dislocates the concerned joint. As soon as the joint is hyperextended, the practitioner may emit explosive energy simultaneously in two parallel and opposite directions. Splitting energy acts outwardly as splitting movements, internally as splitting energy, and, applied to the opponent, as splitting techniques.

Solo exercise

Movements: Assume a *wuji* commencing posture. Make a step forward with the right foot, raise the right hand to shoulder height with the palm facing upward, and push the left hand down with the palm facing downward. At the same time, bend the legs and lower the center of gravity and shift weight to the left foot.

Make a step forward with the left foot, exchange the roles of the two hands, and complete the same exercise. Walk forward by doing further repetitions. (Figures 6.37–6.39)

FIGURE 6.37   FIGURE 6.38

FIGURE 6.39

Partner exercise

Movements: *B* advances and strikes *A* with his left palm. *A* grasps *B*'s left wrist with his left hand, holds *B*'s elbow with his right hand, and at the same time steps forward with his right foot. *A* pushes *B*'s wrist down with his left hand and lifts *B*'s elbow upward with his right hand. When *B*'s left elbow joint is hyperextended, *A* emits explosive energy with his two hands, making *B*'s attack futile. *A* and *B* complete the same exercise with their roles exchanged and do further repetitions of the exercise. (Figures 6.40–6.42)

FIGURE 6.40

FIGURE 6.41

FIGURE 6.42

Efficacy: Splitting energy functions to stop the opponent's attack and to perform seizing and joint-locking. It can hurt the tendons, misplace the bones, and cut energy and *qi*.

Advice: Splitting energy may cause injuries, so it should be applied under strict control to prevent accidents.

The techniques for applying splitting energy also include: splitting the shoulder joints, splitting the neck, splitting the lower back, and splitting the hip joints.

7. Elbow energy

Elbow (*zhou*) energy refers to a technique of hitting the opponent with the point of the elbow or the area around the elbow point when getting near to the opponent. Sometimes the elbow strike may not knock the opponent very far away, but it may effectively stop the opponent's attack because it is characterized with the short distance between the elbow and the target, the strike's small acting area, powerful explosive force, and tremendous penetrability.

In Taiji push-hands and fighting technique, elbow technique is applied under two circumstances. The first circumstance is when a practitioner has to use elbow technique as a remedial act when his fist or palm strike has been neutralized and his first defending line pierced through by the opponent. Elbow attack, like "fighting at close quarters," acts as a reserve force for the fist or the palm. The second circumstance is when a practitioner has to stop the opponent's fist attack or palm attack for protecting the second defending line when the opponent has pierced through the practitioner's first defending line.

There are twenty-four techniques for applying elbow energy, including: single elbow blow, double elbow blow, front elbow blow, elbow blow to the heart, pushing elbow blow, raising elbow blow, rear elbow blow, and pressing elbow blow.

The technical characteristics of elbow energy include the elbow strikes in various directions in a situation in which the intent integrates with *qi* and external movements. Elbow energy acts outwardly as elbow movements, internally as elbow energy, and, applied to the opponent, as elbow techniques.

Solo exercise

Movements: Adopt a *wuji* commencing posture. Step forward with the right foot, raise the right hand to shoulder height, and extend the right arm. After making a clockwise circle with the right hand, change the right palm into a fist. Step forward with the left foot, cross the two arms before the chest with the forearms more or less parallel to the ground and elbows facing outward, shift the center of gravity to the left foot, and hit leftward with the left elbow. Complete the same exercise with the roles of the two elbows exchanged. Walk straight ahead by doing further repetitions of the exercise. (Figures 6.43, 6.44)

FIGURE 6.43   FIGURE 6.44

Partner exercise

Movements: *B* steps out and launches a blow to the chest with his right fist. *A* stretches out his right hand and catches *B*'s right wrist, makes a step forward with his left foot simultaneously, closes his two elbows by dropping the elbows towards his own ribs and centerline, and hits *B*'s right ribs with his left elbow. *A* and *B* complete the same exercise with their roles exchanged and do further repetitions of the exercise. (Figures 6.45–6.47)

FIGURE 6.45

FIGURE 6.46

FIGURE 6.47

Efficacy: Elbow energy has the effects of short applying distance, tiny acting area, powerful explosive force, and tremendous penetrability.

Advice: Elbow energy may injure the opponent, so it should be used under strict control to prevent accidents.

8. Leaning energy

Leaning (*kao*)—or, more descriptively, bumping—energy, backed up by abundant internal energy, is applied when the opponent's body closes in. It is an explosive energy which can be so powerful that it resembles an exploding mountain. It can be an extremely powerful and overwhelming force with the momentum of an avalanche because of its large acting area and comparatively long acting time.

In Taiji push-hands and fighting technique, leaning energy is used under two circumstances. One circumstance is when a practitioner's first attack with his fist or palm and second attack with his elbow as a remedying technique have been neutralized by the opponent. The practitioner then applies leaning energy to continue the attack. At this moment, leaning technique is like a majestic-looking general going into battle in ancient times, whose great momentum is overwhelming. However, if leaning energy is not properly applied, the result will be worse than anything imaginable. Another circumstance is when an opponent has pierced through the practitioner's first and second defending lines and the practitioner has to apply leaning technique to block and to counter-attack. If leaning energy is well applied, the practitioner will change the danger into safety.

Leaning technique is the last defending line of a practitioner. It is vital for a practitioner how well his leaning technique is applied. In the event that the last defending line is pierced through by the opponent, the practitioner will be in great danger.

The techniques to apply leaning energy include: leaning forward with the shoulder, leaning backward with the shoulder, leaning with the head, leaning with the chest, leaning with the back, leaning with the buttock, leaning with the hip, and leaning with the knee.

The technical characteristics of leaning energy include that when the practitioner nestles up against the opponent's body with the intent integrated with *qi* and external movements, he suddenly emits leaning energy aiming at the opponent's center of gravity. Leaning energy acts outwardly as leaning movements, internally as leaning energy, and, applied to the opponent, as leaning techniques.

Solo exercise

Movements: Adopt a *wuji* commencing posture. Make a step forward with the right foot, bend the right knee and press down with the left foot, and shift the center of gravity to the right foot. At the same time, raise the left hand and put it on the front side of the right shoulder with the palm facing outward and lower the right hand beside the right hip with the hand changed into a fist. Then step out with the left foot and complete the same procedure with the roles of the shoulders and hands exchanged. Walk forward by doing further repetitions of the exercise. (Figures 6.48, 6.49)

FIGURE 6.48   FIGURE 6.49

Partner exercise

Movements: *B* makes a step forward with his right foot and punches towards *A*'s chest with his right fist. *A* deflects *B*'s fist with his left hand and takes the opportunity to advance and bump with his right shoulder against the area between *B*'s shoulder and ribs until *B* is bumped away. *A* and *B* complete the same exercise with their roles exchanged and do further repetitions of the exercise. (Figures 6.50–6.53)

Figure 6.50

Figure 6.51

Figure 6.52

FIGURE 6.53

Efficacy: Leaning energy, backed up by a practitioner's abundant internal power, functions as an explosive energy which enables the practitioner to block the opponent's attack effectively and, figuratively speaking, come from behind to win the competition.

Advice: The power of leaning energy comes from abundant internal *qi*, so a practitioner should practice the exercises of internal power (*neigong*) to develop leaning energy and its quality.

Illustration of the eight techniques of Taiji and their directions

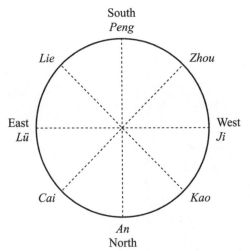

FIGURE 6.54 THE EIGHT TECHNIQUES: THE FOUR CARDINAL DIRECTIONS AND THE FOUR CORNERS

B. COMBINED EXERCISES OF THE THIRTEEN POSTURES OF TAIJI

The thirteen postures of Taiji is a joint name of the eight techniques (warding off, rolling back, pressing, pushing, plucking, splitting, elbow, and leaning) and the five steps (forward, backward, beware of the left, look to the right, and central equilibrium) of Taiji.

1. Warding off

Movements: Assume a *wuji* commencing posture. Make a step forward with the right foot. Raise both hands slowly from the left hip to nose height with warding-off energy in them. Put the right hand in front and the left hand at the rear with the two hands facing forward. Keep the two arms curved and a distance of 30cm between them. At the same time, shift the center of gravity to the right foot and make a stance with the front leg bent and the rear foot pressing down. Look at the direction in which the warding-off technique is applied. (Figures 6.55, 6.56)

FIGURE 6.55   FIGURE 6.56

2. Rolling back

Movements: Continuing from the previous movement, make a circle with both hands and finish it with both hands facing the left. Lead the waist with the two hands and lead the hands with the waist. The two hands slowly roll back horizontally all the way to a position in front of the left shoulder. The right hand stays ahead of the left with both hands facing outward, with the two arms curved like two bows about 30cm apart. In the meantime, gradually shift the center of gravity to the left foot from the right foot and bend the left leg. Then relax and lower the two arms toward the left hip. Look at the direction in which the rolling-back technique is applied. (Figures 6.57, 6.58)

| FIGURE 6.57 | FIGURE 6.58 |

3. Pressing

Movements: Continuing from the previous movement, turn the right foot 45 degrees outward and shift the center of gravity from the left foot to the right foot. Then move the left foot forward and stop beside the right foot with the toes on the ground to make an empty stance. Advance with the left foot and raise the two hands to chest height with the left palm facing inward and the right palm facing outward. The two palms are at a distance of about 20cm from each other. Slowly push forward with both hands until the two arms are naturally straightened and the gap between the two palms is closed. At the same time, shift the center of gravity to the left foot from the right foot and form a left bow step. Look at the direction in which the pressing technique is applied. (Figures 6.59, 6.60)

FIGURE 6.59   FIGURE 6.60

4. Pushing

Movements: Continuing from the previous movement, move the two hands via a curved path to a position in front of the left half of the chest with the hands facing downward and at a distance of about 10cm. Then slowly push downward with both palms while moving the hands slightly to the right, stopping at the right hip, and keeping a distance of about 20cm between the two palms. In the meantime, shift the center of gravity to the right foot from the left foot and bend the right leg. Look at the direction in which the pushing technique is applied. (Figures 6.61, 6.62)

FIGURE 6.61   FIGURE 6.62

5. Plucking

Movements: Continuing from the previous movement, after shifting the center of gravity from the right foot to the left, make a big step forward with the right foot and shift the center of gravity back to the right foot. At the same time, cross the two arms in front of the body and then part the two arms to shoulder width while raising them until they approach a level slightly higher than the shoulders. At this point, the arms are straightened naturally and the palms are facing downward. Clench the fingers and pluck with the two fists downward and back. At the same time, quickly step backward with the right foot to a position in front of the left foot, bend the left leg, and shift the center of gravity to the left foot. Look at the direction in which the plucking technique is applied. (Figures 6.63–6.65)

FIGURE 6.63

FIGURE 6.64

FIGURE 6.65

6. Splitting

Movements: Continuing from the previous movement, make a step forward with the left foot and raise the right hand to a position at the level of the left elbow with the right palm facing downward and the distance between the hands being about 50cm. Then hold up the left palm and push suddenly down with the right palm. Look at the direction in which the splitting technique is applied and lower the center of gravity. (Figures 6.66, 6.67)

FIGURE 6.66   FIGURE 6.67

7. Elbow

Movements: Continuing from the previous movement, relax and lower both hands and then raise the right arm to shoulder level until the arm is naturally straightened. While clenching the fingers, make a clockwise circle with the right fist around the right wrist. Make a big step forward with the right foot and launch an elbow strike forward with the right elbow, with the heart of the right fist facing inward. In the meantime, move the left fist toward the left hip with the heart of the left fist facing upward. Lower the center of gravity and form a right bow step. Look at the direction in which the elbow technique is applied. (Figures 6.68, 6.69)

FIGURE 6.68

FIGURE 6.69

8. Leaning

Movements: Continuing from the previous movement, relax and lower the right elbow. Make a big step forward with the left foot and put the left fist behind the left buttock and the right palm inside the left shoulder with the palm facing leftward. Shift the center of gravity to the left foot to form a left bow step. Look at the direction in which the leaning technique is applied. (Figures 6.70, 6.71)

FIGURE 6.70

FIGURE 6.71

Seven Training Methods for Taiji Push-Hands and Fighting Technique

The various training methods for Taiji push-hands and fighting technique are derived from the principles expressed in the theory of Taijiquan: "adhere/connect/stick/follow; no separation, no forcing (through); no excess, no deficiency; follow, bend, then extend." The training methods make use of the thirteen postures of Taiji, namely warding off (*peng*), rolling back (*lü*), pressing (*ji*), pushing (*an*), plucking (*cai*), splitting (*lie*), elbow (*zhou*), leaning (*kao*), step forward (*jin bu*), step backward (*tui bu*), beware of the left (*zuo gu*), look to the right (*you pan*), and central equilibrium (*zhong ding*).

The training will, through the method of listening energy (*ting jin*), improve the sensitivity of the whole-body tactile and internal sensations. The improved sensitivity will allow you to develop the Taiji techniques of "give up yourself and follow the opponent," "guide the opponent to enter into emptiness," "take advantage of the opponent's momentum and borrow his force," "control the heavy with the light," and "use four ounces to deflect one thousand pounds."

A. TRAINING STEPS
1. *Three stages of learning Taiji push-hands*
Stage 1: Improving external movements
A newcomer to Taiji push-hands should pay attention to all parts of his body and make them meet the requirements of the movements. The movements of Taiji form and push-hands are designed according to the structure of the human body and related closely with the circulating routes of the internal

qi. Therefore, performing the movements of Taiji form and push-hands correctly is very important, and it is also considered foundational training.

Taiji push-hands is different from Taiji form movement because it is designed as a partner exercise. Therefore, in push-hands, a practitioner should not only complete his own movements correctly and skillfully, but also cooperate with the partner. Both sides should coordinate their movements and follow each other. While conducting the techniques of adhere/connect/stick/follow and listening energy in line with the principles of "no separating, no forcing; no tilting, no resisting," a practitioner should strive to make his movements round, full, soft, and smooth. The movements should not be broken by any protruding, dented, flawed, intermittent, or stiff segments.

Stage 2: Cultivating energy

The main exercise at this stage is to apply the various energies (*jin*) learned in Taijiquan form movement to push-hands practice for adjusting and mastering the proper extent of usage. The recommended approach is that *A* applies the form of energy being trained to *B*, whereas *B* acts to "feed energy" (i.e., to cooperatively serve energy) to *A*. The training continues with the same roles for some time and then the roles are switched. No other exercises should be practiced until this exercise is done correctly and skillfully.

A major point at this stage is that the practice should not only include the energies learned from Taijiquan forms but also the energies that cannot be experienced in form movement. A primary goal is to obtain, through push-hands practice, rational knowledge of the various energies felt during form play.

Stage 3: Understanding energy

At the stage of exercising to understand energy, the training progresses to both parties attacking and defending (and neutralizing) without the predetermined roles of the previous stage, by which the training partners pursue understanding energy. Meanwhile, both sides learn from experience how to pit the weak against the strong, how to use four ounces to deflect one thousand pounds, and how to gain victory by ingenuity.

Whenever there is "separation, tilting, forcing, or resisting" or "double-heaviness," a practitioner should learn how to apply body work, foot techniques, and/or hand techniques to adjust and correct the problem.

In attack, when a practitioner gets his fist(s) or foot out of the first defending line, he should learn how to apply elbow techniques or knee techniques to attack; when the practitioner gets his elbow or knee out of the second defending line, he should know how to apply shoulder techniques to attack. The same applies in defense.

The above outlines the stage of understanding energy. Because of their different levels of skill in push-hands, practitioners will also have different levels of understanding energy. For example, a practitioner at the level of moving-step push-hands must have a higher level of understanding energy than a practitioner at the level of fixed-step push-hands. Similarly, a practitioner at the level of free fighting must have a higher level of understanding energy than a practitioner at the level of push-hands. In short, there is no limit to the development of one's technique.

2. Proper distance

Before starting a push-hands exercise, both practitioners should first stand face to face. The two should then make fists and raise their hands forward to shoulder height until their arms are fully extended. The distance between the two is considered proper for push-hands when their fists can barely touch. Additionally, each practitioner should stand in a centered, upright, calm, and comfortable posture and look towards the opponent's face. (Figure 7.1)

FIGURE 7.1

B. SINGLE-HANDED PUSH-HANDS EXERCISES WITH FIXED STEPS

1. Single-handed push-hands exercise I

Movement 1: Both *A* and *B* make a step forward with their right feet, so that the transverse distance between the feet will be about 15cm. Both practitioners extend their right arms simultaneously and make the backs of their hands touch at abdomen height. Each practitioner looks towards the opponent. (Figure 7.2)

FIGURE 7.2

Movement 2: *A* leads *B*'s right arm to make a horizontal clockwise circle. Each practitioner's center of gravity shifts from one foot to the other following the circling movement. Then further repetitions of the movement should be done. (Figure 7.3)

FIGURE 7.3

Movement 3: *B* leads *A*'s right arm to complete the same exercise in the reverse direction. Further repetitions of this movement should be done as well. Then the practitioners withdraw their right feet, make a step forward with their left feet, and extend their left arms to do the same exercise on the left side. (Figure 7.4)

FIGURE 7.4

Characteristics: The intent (*yi*) is round; the external movements are round; and *qi* is round. The internal and the external conform to each other.

Advice: A practitioner should master the principle of circular movements, and be perfectly arched and smooth everywhere so that his balance will not be destroyed under the influence of intruding forces. There should not be any weak points, in any situation and at any angle, of which the opponent may take advantage.

At the same time, a practitioner should gradually learn how to destroy the opponent's balance in all situations and at all angles. This kind of skill is difficult to master and deserves long-term training.

Making circles in single-handed or double-handed push-hands is the basic technique for improving a practitioner's Taiji push-hands skills. For beginners, the circles should be made larger than usual, and along the circle there should be no uneven, flawed, or intermittent parts and there should be no forcing or resisting. The level marked by round intent, round external movements, and round *qi* will be gradually reached after a long period of practice.

2. Single-handed push-hands exercise II

Movement 1: Both *A* and *B* make a step forward with their right feet, so that the transverse distance between the feet will be about 15 cm. Both practitioners keep their left hands on their hips, extend their right arms simultaneously, and make the backs of their right hands touch at abdomen height. The two practitioners look towards each other. (Figure 7.5)

FIGURE 7.5

Movement 2: *A* leads *B*'s arm to make a vertical circle clockwise around the anteroposterior axis which runs horizontally through the front and back of their bodies. Each practitioner's center of gravity shifts from one foot to the other following the circling movement. Then further repetitions of the movement should be done. (Figure 7.6)

FIGURE 7.6

Movement 3: *B* leads *A*'s right arm to complete the same exercise in the reverse direction. Further repetitions of this movement should be done as well. Then the practitioners withdraw their right feet, make a step forward with their left feet, and extend their left arms to do the same exercise on the left side. (Figure 7.7)

FIGURE 7.7

Characteristics: Adhere/connect/stick/follow and listening energy are important techniques of Taiji push-hands and a unique training method. Beginners are advised to start with the primary exercises of adhere/connect/stick/follow and listening energy (see Section A in Chapter VIII).

Advice: Beginners should do the movements slowly. Slow practice enables the practitioner to take care that every part of his body moves in unison and according to the six harmonies. Additionally, slow practice also enables the practitioner to detect flaws in his own movement, such as uneven, flawed, or intermittent parts or forcing or resisting. Practitioners benefit from slow practice in correcting mistakes.

3. Single-handed push-hands exercise III

Movement 1: Both *A* and *B* make a step forward with their right feet, so that the transverse distance between the feet will be about 15cm. Both practitioners extend their right arms simultaneously and make the backs of their hands touch at abdomen height. Each practitioner looks towards the opponent. (Figure 7.8)

FIGURE 7.8

Movement 2: *A* leads *B*'s hand along a vertical circle around a horizontal axis paralleling their chests at chest level. The center of gravity of each practitioner shifts between the two feet accordingly. Repeat the same exercise several times. (Figure 7.9)

FIGURE 7.9

Movement 3: *B* leads *A*'s right arm to complete the same exercise in the reverse direction. Repeat the exercise several times. Then each practitioner withdraws his right foot, makes a step forward with his left foot, and stretches his left arm out to complete the same exercise. (Figure 7.10)

FIGURE 7.10

Characteristics: See the previous exercise.

Advice: Practicing Taiji push-hands has certain rules, and beginners should pay attention to them while exercising and correct mistakes as soon as they are detected. Focus should be put on correcting improper postures and energy in order to make all movements gradually meet the requirements of Taiji push-hands. It might not seem like a quick way to make progress, but a practitioner, in doing so, can make steady progress step by step as he masters the basic techniques. Furthermore, a practitioner can lay a solid foundation for reaching an advanced stage of "breaking away from the rules while conforming to the rules" in the long run.

C. SINGLE-HANDED PUSH-HANDS EXERCISES WITH MOVING STEPS

1. Single-handed silk-reeling push-hands exercise

Movement 1: Both *A* and *B* make a step forward with their right feet, so that the transverse distance between the feet will be about 15cm. Both practitioners extend their right arms simultaneously and make the backs of the hands touch each other at shoulder height. Each practitioner looks towards the opponent. (Figure 7.11)

FIGURE 7.11

Movement 2: *A* steps forward, moves his right arm spirally towards *B*'s right hip, and lowers his center of gravity. *B* withdraws by stepping back, following *A*'s movement, and lowers his center of gravity as well. (Figure 7.12)

Figure 7.12

Movement 3: *B* steps forward, raises his right arm, and moves it spirally towards *A*'s right hip while lowering his center of gravity. *A* withdraws by stepping back, following *B*'s movement, and lowers his center of gravity. After doing further repetitions, the exercise should be done from the left side. (Figure 7.13)

Figure 7.13

Characteristics: Silk-reeling in the *shun* and *ni* directions ("going with" and "going against"); also spiraling, turning, twining, and rotating.

Advice: See Section D in this chapter.

2. Single-handed push-hands exercise alternating between attack and neutralization

Movement 1: Both *A* and *B* make a step forward with their right feet, so that the transverse distance between the feet will be about 15cm. Both practitioners extend their right arms simultaneously and make the backs of their hands touch at shoulder level. Each practitioner looks towards the opponent. (Figure 7.14)

FIGURE 7.14

Movement 2: *A* makes an outward-facing "standing palm" (fingers pointing up, palm not squarely facing forward) and tries to push *B* on the central position of the body. *B* withdraws his right foot, turns his chest, and rotates his right hand to lead *A*'s hand to the right and downwards to neutralize *A*'s attack. (Figure 7.15a)

FIGURE 7.15A

Movement 3: *B* makes an outward-facing "standing palm" and tries to push *A* on the central position of the body. *A* withdraws his right foot, turns his chest, and makes a curve with his right hand to lead *B*'s hand to the right and downward to neutralize *B*'s attack. The center of gravity of each practitioner shifts between the two feet following the advancing and retreating movements. After doing further repetitions, the exercise should be done from the left side. (Figure 7.15b)

FIGURE 7.15B

Characteristics: This exercise is a process of attack and neutralization that exercises "using softness to beat hardness," "giving up oneself and following the opponent," and "guiding the opponent to enter into emptiness."

Advice: Some trainees make the movements of the exercise correctly, but the movements do not have the expected effect. Without powerful, light, and agile internal power (*neigong*), it will be difficult for a trainee to lead and move the opponent or to emit force clearly, even though the trainee may make the correct movements and have a sensitive tactile sensation. On the contrary, it is easy for the trainee to be led and controlled by the opponent.

A practitioner cannot launch a powerful attack, neutralize the intruding energy, or make a good emission of energy without being supported by sufficient internal energy. The practitioner may originally try to guide the intruding energy of the opponent, but, on the contrary, the centered and upright position of his body may be lost. In the words of the ancients: "Learning to move is easy; learning *gongfu* is hard." Only a high standard of *gongfu* will lead to moves that satisfy a practitioner himself and are admired by the opponent.

3. Single-handed push-hands exercise with circle walking

Movement 1: *A* and *B* stand face to face with a distance of two arms' length between them. With their left hands on their hips, both *A* and *B* extend their right arms simultaneously and make the backs of the hands touch. Each practitioner looks towards the opponent. (Figure 7.16)

FIGURE 7.16

Movement 2: Both *A* and *B* walk along a clockwise circle while making clockwise circles with their right arms. Each practitioner lowers his center of gravity and shifts it between his two feet with the stepping. After doing further repetitions, the exercise should be done from the left side. (Figures 7.17, 7.18)

FIGURE 7.17

FIGURE 7.18

Characteristics: The upper and the lower coordinate with each other. The hand, body, and foot techniques are utilized in harmony.

Advice: Single-handed push-hands exercise with circle walking is designed to further improve the coordination between the upper and the lower, and the harmony between the hand, foot, and body techniques following on from the single-handed fixed-step push-hands exercises. The requirements of the stepping method in Taiji push-hands are that the substantial and the insubstantial should be clear when transforming between going forward and backward, the body should turn following the waist while moving forward or backward, and the feet should move in an agile manner and land stably in order to support the movements well and keep the center of gravity stable.

D. DOUBLE-HANDED PUSH-HANDS EXERCISES WITH FIXED STEPS

1. Basic exercise of double-handed push-hands

Movement 1: Both *A* and *B* make a step forward with their right feet, so that the transverse distance between the feet will be about 15cm. Both practitioners extend their right arms simultaneously and make the backs of the hands touch while also touching each other's right elbows with their left hands. (Figure 7.19)

FIGURE 7.19

Movement 2: Both *A* and *B* make a clockwise circle with their arms. The center of gravity of each practitioner shifts between his legs along with the movement. Further repetitions of the movement are done. (Figure 7.20)

FIGURE 7.20

Movement 3: *A* and *B* make a counterclockwise circle. After further repetitions of this movement, the exercise should be done from the left side. (Figure 7.21)

FIGURE 7.21

Characteristics: When circular movements have been mastered, the circles can be made perfectly round and natural, and balance can be maintained under the impact of an intruding force.

Advice: This primary stage is the breaking-in stage where both sides try to move cooperatively. Movements of the two practitioners are required to adhere/connect/stick/follow, to not separate or fight force head on, and to make perfect round movements without any uneven, flawed, or intermittent parts in order to reach the state of harmony.

2. Double-handed silk-reeling push-hands exercise

Movement 1: Both *A* and *B* make a step forward with their right feet, so that the transverse distance between the feet will be about 15cm. Both practitioners extend their right arms simultaneously and make the backs of the hands touch while also touching each other's right elbows with their left hands at chest level. Each practitioner looks towards the opponent. (Figure 7.22)

FIGURE 7.22

Movement 2: *A* leads *B*'s arm to make a clockwise spiral rotation and repeats the movement. Each practitioner's center of gravity shifts between his feet following the movement. (Figure 7.23)

FIGURE 7.23

Movement 3: *B* leads *A*'s arm to make counterclockwise spiral rotations. After further repetitions of the movement, they withdraw their right feet and step out with their left feet, and then do the same exercise from the left side. (Figure 7.24)

FIGURE 7.24

Characteristics: This exercise represents a transition from the large circles of the single-handed silk-reeling push-hands exercise to circles that are middle-sized. In Taiji theory, this development is stated as "pursuing large movements first; then pursuing small and well-knit movements."

Advice: When a practitioner has exercised the double-handed silk-reeling push-hands exercise well and developed the ability to make all parts of his body rotate whenever one part rotates, he has reached a state in which "the internal and the external echo each other and act in unison." At this stage, there are external circles made by the hands, elbows, shoulders, chest, abdomen, waist, hips, knees, and feet, and there are also internal rotations made by the internal *qi* that follow the external circles. This stage is a step in the progression of silk-reeling skill where large circles change into middle-sized ones and middle circles change into small ones.

When a practitioner has, through practicing silk-reeling, changed small circles into invisible ones and reached a level where the internal energy spirals internally, he is then considered to have reached an advanced stage of Taiji push-hands where visible movements change into invisible and intangible movements.

E. DOUBLE-HANDED PUSH-HANDS EXERCISES WITH MOVING STEPS

1. Double-handed push-hands exercise alternating between attack and neutralization

Movement 1: *A* and *B* stand face to face and look at each other at a distance of about one arm's length. *A* makes a step forward with his right foot and, with his right hand, tries to push the left side of *B*'s chest, whereas *B* makes a step backward with his left foot, raises his left hand to meet *A*'s right hand, and neutralizes the push. At the same time, *B* turns his waist and chest to the left to support his neutralizing energy. (Figures 7.25, 7.26)

FIGURE 7.25

FIGURE 7.26

Movement 2: *A* makes a step forward with his left foot and, with his left hand, tries to push the right side of *B*'s chest. *B* makes a step backward with his left foot, raises his right hand to meet *A*'s pushing hand, and then neutralizes the push. At the same time, *B* turns his chest and waist to the right to support his neutralizing energy. Each practitioner's center of gravity shifts between their feet along with the forward/backward stepping. After doing further repetitions of the exercise, and effectively walking in one direction, *A* and *B* exchange their roles. (Figures 7.27, 7.28)

FIGURE 7.27

FIGURE 7.28

Characteristics: "Adhere/connect/stick/follow," "No separation or fighting force head on," "Give up yourself and follow the opponent," and "Guide the opponent to enter into emptiness."

Advice: To learn Taiji push-hands, the primary stage for a practitioner is to start with soft and slow movements. After having exercised for a period of time, laying a solid foundation, he may do the exercise at variable speed. The practitioner should be able to move fast or slow according to the opponent's movements. It is a weakness in fighting technique if a practitioner does not have the ability to meet an emergency promptly. In this case, he can neither deal with the opponent's quick attack nor launch a quick attack or retreat.

Therefore, Wang Zongyue maintained: "React quickly when the opponent moves quickly, whereas follow slowly when the opponent moves slowly"; Chen Xin's view was: "Spiraling or rotation should be extremely fast." No training method in the Taiji classics suggests moving at an absolute even speed in exercises. In line with the dialectical law, "Conduct energy like reeling silk" expresses that movements can be slow, whereas "Emit energy like shooting an arrow" expresses that movements can be very fast.

2. Double-handed push-hands exercise in four directions

Movement 1: See Movement 1 in the previous exercise.

Movement 2: See Movement 2 in the previous exercise.

Movement 3: *A* grasps *B*'s right wrist with his right hand, holds *B*'s right elbow with his left hand, and then rolls back *B*'s right arm. At the same time, *A* rotates to the right from the waist, following the rolling-back movement, and takes a step backward with his right foot, shifting his center of gravity to the right foot. (Figure 7.29)

FIGURE 7.29

Movement 4: *B* yields and follows *A*'s movement to get closer and puts his left hand on his right forearm to push *A*'s chest or abdomen. (Figure 7.30)

FIGURE 7.30

Movement 5: Changing from rolling back into pushing down, *A* pushes *B*'s right arm downward with both hands and simultaneously lowers his center of gravity. (Figure 7.31)

FIGURE 7.31

Movement 6: After the beginning circle, *A* and *B* do the above movements with exchanged roles, that is to say, *B* rolls *A*'s arm back, *A* tries to push *B*, and *B* pushes *A* down. After further repetitions of the exercise, it should be done from the other side as well.

Characteristics: See Section A in Chapter VI concerning warding-off energy, rolling-back energy, pressing energy, and pushing energy.

Advice: Double-handed push-hands of the four cardinal directions is an exercise designed to transform the four major energies practitioners learned from practicing Taijiquan forms into practical use via push-hands. Therefore, we need to act in accordance with the experience of our predecessors: "Be conscientious about warding off, rolling back, pressing, and pushing. Make the upper and the lower follow each other, and it will be difficult for the opponent to invade."

When the opponent uses warding-off energy, you can use rolling-back energy to respond; when the opponent uses rolling-back energy, you can counter with pressing energy; and when the opponent employs pressing energy, you can win by making use of pushing energy. In short, between two people doing push-hands, there is simultaneous attacking and defending, emitting and neutralization, and yin and yang mutually creating and subduing one another with endless variation.

F. DOUBLE-HANDED PUSH-HANDS EXERCISES WITH SINGLE-SIDED STEPS

1. Double-handed push-hands exercise with single-sided steps (da lü)

Movement 1: *A* makes a step forward with his right foot while *B* makes a step forward with his left foot, which makes their lower legs touch each other. Each practitioner shifts his center of gravity to the front foot. They both bring the backs of their right hands in contact and put their left hands on the opponent's right elbow. (Figure 7.32)

FIGURE 7.32

Movement 2: *A* uses circular movements to move his right hand downward to touch *B*'s left elbow and his left hand upward to meet the back of *B*'s left hand; *B* does the same to *A*, and thus their combined movement becomes a clockwise circle. At the same time, their front legs that are in contact make a clockwise circle as well. (Figure 7.33)

FIGURE 7.33

Movement 3: *A* rolls *B*'s right arm backward while grasping *B*'s right wrist with his right hand and holding *B*'s right elbow with his left hand. At the same time, *A* rolls *B*'s right leg with his left leg and shifts his weight to his right foot. (Figure 7.34)

FIGURE 7.34

Movement 4: By "giving up oneself and following the opponent," *B* follows *A*'s rolling-back movement and puts his left hand on his right forearm to push *A* on the area of the chest and abdomen. (Figure 7.35)

FIGURE 7.35

Movement 5: *A* changes his energy from rolling back into pushing down on *B*'s pushing right arm and lowers his center of gravity. (Figure 7.36)

FIGURE 7.36

Movement 6: *A* makes a step forward with his right foot and touches *B*'s right leg with his right leg, whereas *B* makes a step backward with his right foot and the same exercise is then done counterclockwise. Further repetitions of the whole exercise are then done. (Figure 7.37)

FIGURE 7.37

Characteristics: The double-handed push-hands exercise with single-sided steps is an exercise practiced by the Chen stylists. It is characterized by circular movement with adhere/connect/stick/follow: circles of the hands in the upper part and circles of the legs in the lower part. The double-handed push-hands exercise with single-sided steps is famed for its techniques of "large rolling back" (*da lü*) and "large leaning" (*da kao*), and thus it is also called "large rolling back (*da lü*) push-hands."

Advice: While doing the exercise, the center of gravity should not be too low, or else warding-off energy will be lost, movements and *qi* obstructed, and there will be stagnation of *qi*.

2. Double-handed push-hands exercise in four directions

Movements 1–5: In this exercise, Movements 1–5 are the same as in the double-handed push-hands exercise with single-sided steps.

Movement 6: With his right hand, *A* grasps *B*'s right wrist and puts his left hand on *B*'s right elbow, whereas *B* puts his left hand on the inside of his own right elbow. Each of the two raises his outer leg. *A* leads *B* eastward. After taking several steps, they turn and *A*'s right leg meets *B*'s left leg. Then they do Movements 1–5 again. (Figure 7.38)

FIGURE 7.38

Movement 7: *B* leads *A* westward. After taking several steps, they repeat Movements 1–5. Also, they do the same exercise in the east and the north. Further repetitions of the whole exercise are then done. (Figure 7.39)

FIGURE 7.39

Characteristics: The five steps of Taijiquan, namely forward, backward, beware of the left, look to the right, and central equilibrium, are practiced in this exercise.

Advice: See Section C in Chapter III.

3. Double-handed push-hands exercise with circle walking

Movements 1–5: In this exercise, Movements 1–5 are the same as in the double-handed push-hands exercise with single-sided steps.

Movement 6: *A* grasps *B*'s right wrist with his right hand and puts his left hand on *B*'s right elbow, whereas *B* puts his left hand on the inside of his own right elbow. *A* advances with his left foot and *B* takes a step back with his left foot. *A* leads *B* to walk around a circle, and after they have made one revolution, *A*'s left leg meets *B*'s right leg and they repeat Movements 1–5. (Figure 7.40)

FIGURE 7.40

Movement 7: *A* and *B* exchange the movements of their hands and legs and they also exchange directions, and then *B* leads *A* to make a revolution around the circle. Then they repeat Movements 1–5. Further repetitions of the whole exercise are then done. (Figure 7.41)

FIGURE 7.41

Characteristics: Building on the basis of the double-handed push-hands exercise with single-sided steps and the double-handed push-hands exercise in four directions, this exercise integrates seizing and joint-locking and throwing out the opponent with the circle walking double-handed push-hands exercise.

Advice: See Section E in Chapter II.

G. FREE PUSH-HANDS EXERCISES

Movements: After practicing the basics of double-handed push-hands for a while, the exercise of free push-hands can be practiced. Free push-hands is done without any specific fixed movements. (Figures 7.42–7.44)

FIGURE 7.42

FIGURE 7.43

FIGURE 7.44

Characteristics: Both sides bring all techniques and types of energy learned from push-hands into full play without any restrictions except that all movements should be performed in line with the principle of adhere/connect/stick/follow.

Advice: In Taiji push-hands, each and every movement has its specific martial application. However, theoretical knowledge of the applications cannot be taken as having the ability to perform them correctly. It makes no sense to mechanically practice fixed application patterns. Instead, we should learn to apply the various movements and energies learned from push-hands to free push-hands and free fighting (sparring).

H. TAIJI FREE-FIGHTING TECHNIQUES
1. *Spring energy*
B (younger, on the right) suddenly rushes at *A*. (Figure 7.45)

FIGURE 7.45

With his hands, *B* forcefully pushes *A*'s upper arms. (Figure 7.46)

FIGURE 7.46

A complies with the momentum of the push and moves his body backward, shifting his center of gravity from the right foot to the left foot. (Figure 7.47)

FIGURE 7.47

A neutralizes *B*'s energy by applying the method of "moving backward before moving forward." (Figure 7.48)

FIGURE 7.48

When the energy in *B*'s movement is gone and he has not generated new energy, *A* changes from defense into attack and employs "spring energy" to pitch *B* out. (Figures 7.49–7.52)

FIGURE 7.49

Figure 7.50

Figure 7.51

Figure 7.52

2. Leg technique

B makes a step forward with his right foot and punches, with his right fist, the left half of *A*'s chest. (Figure 7.53)

FIGURE 7.53

A uses his left hand to deflect and neutralize *B*'s punch. (Figure 7.54)

FIGURE 7.54

A raises his right hand to reach *B*'s neck. (Figures 7.55, 7.56; left/right reversed)

FIGURE 7.55

FIGURE 7.56

At the same time, *A* moves his right foot forward, placing it against the outside of *B*'s left leg. (Figure 7.57; left/right reversed)

FIGURE 7.57

With his right foot, *A* kicks *B*'s left leg, and simultaneously crosscuts *B*'s neck with his right palm. (Figure 7.58)

FIGURE 7.58

B falls down. (Figures 7.59, 7.60)

Figure 7.59

Figure 7.60

3. Silk-reeling skill

B, with his right hand, grabs *A*'s right wrist and places his left hand on *A*'s right elbow. (Figure 7.61)

FIGURE 7.61

B turns and twists *A*'s right arm in order to apply a joint-locking technique. (Figure 7.62)

FIGURE 7.62

A employs silk-reeling to spiral his right arm. (Figure 7.63)

FIGURE 7.63

A frees himself of *B*'s joint-locking attempt. (Figure 7.64)

FIGURE 7.64

A applies a counter joint-locking technique. (Figure 7.65)

FIGURE 7.65

A completes the counter joint-locking technique. (Figure 7.66)

FIGURE 7.66

A presses *B* down. (Figure 7.67)

FIGURE 7.67

A follows *B*'s movement and throws *B* to the ground. (Figure 7.68)

FIGURE 7.68

4. Turning from the waist

B takes a step forward with his right foot and, with his right hand, delivers a punch to the left side of *A*'s chest. *A* raises his left hand to meet the punch. (Figure 7.69)

FIGURE 7.69

With his left hand, *A* deflects and neutralizes *B*'s punch. (Figure 7.70)

FIGURE 7.70

A takes advantage of the situation to get close to *B*. (Figure 7.71)

FIGURE 7.71

Using his right hand, *A* takes hold of *B*'s neck. (Figure 7.72)

FIGURE 7.72

A pulls *B*'s neck with his right hand and pushes *B*'s right arm with his left hand. (Figures 7.73, 7.74)

FIGURE 7.73

FIGURE 7.74

Turning from the waist, *A* lifts *B* and makes him flip over and fall to the ground. (Figures 7.75, 7.76)

FIGURE 7.75

FIGURE 7.76

—— CHAPTER VIII ——

Essence of Taiji Energies

There are various energies (*jin*) in Taijiquan. Broadly, they can be divided into two categories: visible energies and invisible energies. The visible energies can be seen, and they are easy to understand and master in practice; whereas the invisible energies, hiding inside, cannot be seen, and they are difficult to understand or master. For example, many key techniques, including adhere/connect/stick/follow, listening energy, neutralizing energy, inquiring energy, leading the opponent to enter and fall into emptiness, and deflecting one thousand pounds with four ounces, can only really be experienced, understood, and mastered through practice of Taiji push-hands or fighting techniques.

A. ADHERE/CONNECT/STICK/FOLLOW AND LISTENING ENERGY

The technique of adhere/connect/stick/follow is a unique training method in Taiji push-hands. As the practitioners touch each other in push-hands, the application of the thirteen techniques of Taiji is exercised through adhere/connect/stick/follow and listening energy.

Taiji push-hands is not only the process of the employment of the thirteen techniques of Taiji, but also a process of adhere/connect/stick/follow, and further a process of listening energy that permeates the entire process of push-hands. On the one hand, listening energy makes adhere/connect/stick/follow possible, but on the other hand, it can be said that there will not be listening energy without adhere/connect/stick/follow. The relationship between adhere/connect/stick/follow and listening energy is that they are mutually indispensable to each other; they depend on each other and compensate each other.

The prerequisite for listening energy is that the practitioner should be in contact with the opponent's body and/or limbs as well as the opponent's energy. Then he may detect the opponent's internal and external changes so as to analyze and judge the opponent's intention, force, directions, paths, and angles. In this way he can make the decision to attack or defend.

When a practitioner uses listening energy very skillfully, he can reach a level at which one can learn, without the slightest error, the magnitude and reach of the incoming force.

How can a practitioner determine the proper moment and use listening energy appropriately? While practicing push-hands, one should neither lose nor resist the opponent, and one also should not over-yield during adhere/connect/stick/follow. One should abandon oneself and follow the opponent. No matter how much the opponent changes his energy or its directions, one should not depart from the key principles.

One should glue oneself strongly to the contact points on the opponent's body or limbs. The absorption should be so strong that the opponent can never break free. The part of one's body or limbs stuck on the opponent should act as an adhesive disc and a monitor to probe, at any moment, all the changes the opponent may make internally or externally. Well-trained people can even feel the opponent's breath, pulse rhythm, and changes in pulse; much like a Chinese traditional medicine doctor who diagnoses a patient by feeling the pulse.

One of the important roles played by adhere/connect/stick/follow and listening energy is that they enable one to take preventive measures at the right time, so that the opponent can neither deploy listening energy accurately and act in a timely way, nor employ his techniques properly or use his skills to the full extent. Armed with listening energy, one can conduct adhere/connect/stick/follow when trying to detect the opponent's weak points. When the opponent's weak points and changes in his force point have been detected, one can lead the opponent's center of gravity in, make his body and force enter into emptiness, and pitch him out using the tactics of emitting whenever the neutralization has been done.

The purpose of listening energy is to use stillness to control motion and to attack late but control the opponent. In push-hands, if the opponent greatly changes his movements, you should change greatly; if he makes changes slightly, you should change slightly. One should follow according to the opponent's attack, regardless of the direction, route, or angle. One should "learn the opponent externally through watching and hearing and learn him internally through adhere/connect/stick/follow." When a practitioner is able to do all this, it means he has reached the stage of understanding energy at which he does push-hands without separation, blockage, resistance, or over-yielding. That is why the training of listening energy is considered the only pathway to understanding energy.

An important part of mastering listening energy is learning to relax. A practitioner can develop listening energy in coordination with adhere/connect/stick/follow and the thirteen techniques of Taiji. Relaxation helps promote the reactive abilities of the practitioner's Zang-organs, muscles, skin, joints, and various nerve systems. If a practitioner's spirit, mind, muscles, skin, or joints are tense or rigid, he will not only have poor listening energy, but also slow reactions and stubborn energy, or even worse, he will make mistakes like *diu/pian/ding/kang* (see Chapter II). Therefore, it is emphasized in Taiji classics that "each section should be relaxed, hair should stand on end, the entire body should be threaded up, and the insubstantial and agility should exist inside."

Also, relaxation can make *qi* descend down to the *dantian*, lower the center of gravity, increase the power of the legs and *gongfu* of the lower section, and promote the combination of the internal and the external and the external response to the internal. A light, agile, heavy, and malleable inner energy will be cultivated gradually after long-term exercise on relaxation.

Inner energy will make the skin more sensitive. Sharper sensitivity will help automatically neutralize the intruding energy emitted by the opponent, or minimize its effect. Therefore, neutralizing energy can be developed and can function well as long as the sensitivity of muscles and skin has been adequately improved.

In contrast, the practitioner can detect nothing about the opponent in push-hands, just like walking with his face muffled, if his listening energy has not yet developed well.

Generally speaking, there are two reasons which make a practitioner fail to develop a good skill in listening energy. One of the two reasons is that the contact between two practitioners is too tight, which blunts sensitivity and makes reactions slow, forces rigid, and ability to make changes retarded. Another reason is that the contact is too loose, which results in the mistake of "losing energy." Losing energy happens when the two sides fail to stick to the opponent's body and limbs or when they fail to follow the changes in the opponent's energy because they have not mastered the techniques of adhere/connect/stick/follow so that they separate from each other. For example, in push-hands, one party might be leading and rolling back the other party and the other party stays unmoved or even pulls backward so that the parties separate at the position they touched.

It is called "losing physically" to separate physically from the opponent. It is called "losing energy" when one cannot follow the opponent's energy. Losing physically is a more serious mistake than losing energy is.

To progress in push-hands, a practitioner should devote a lot of time and energy to improve his adhere/connect/stick/follow and listening energy. In full possession of listening energy, a practitioner is able to learn the origin and development of the opponent's energy, cultivate listening energy that enables a state in which "the opponent does not know me, but I know the opponent," and neutralize various types of intruding energy accordingly, which means that the practitioner masters a high standard of *gongfu* with which "a feather cannot be added and a fly cannot land."

To summarize, adhere/connect/stick/follow provides us with an important way to cultivate listening energy, whereas listening energy is the only technique which must be developed and a basic skill to detect the opponent's intention and scout the opponent's energy. The following are the four stages a practitioner has to go through to acquire listening energy.

First stage: Bone sensitivity

The stage of bone sensitivity refers to the situation in which a beginner cannot sense the intruding energy accurately and in a timely way, until the energy penetrates his skin and muscles and reaches the bones. At this stage, the practitioner often adopts a passive position and gets involved in a bull– bull fight, that is, force against force.

At this stage, a practitioner is trained to remove the rigidity existing in his joints and muscles. A practitioner gradually resorts less and less to bull–bull fighting as he utilizes the techniques of Taiji push-hands more and more skillfully.

Second stage: Muscle sensitivity

The stage of muscle sensitivity refers to the situation in which, at the moment the intruding energy hits the muscles, a practitioner can feel and discern, employing listening energy, the strength, direction, and speed of the energy, as well as its alternation between substantial and insubstantial or between curved and straight. Also, he is able to get hold of the opportunities and rhythm to lead, neutralize, hold, and emit.

As long as the practitioner masters the techniques of this level, then, just as a traditional Chinese medicine doctor "feels pulse," he can distinctly learn the changes between yin and yang, and insubstantial and substantial, through a slight touch on the patient's wrist.

Third stage: Skin and hair sensitivity

The stage of skin and hair sensitivity means that both sides feel changes in the opponent's energy depending on his tactile sensation of the skin, which indicates that his level of listening energy has reached a high standard. He detects and judges the opponent's situation totally relying on his nerve endings and listening energy, which is a conditional reflex. This conditional reflex has been developed during his long-term push-hands practice.

At this stage, the practitioner's level can be rated as advanced in push-hands. He can experience the situations in which "when the opponent does not move, I do not move; when the opponent is about to move, I move first" and "a feather cannot be added and a fly cannot land."

Fourth stage: Qi sensitivity

In Taiji push-hands or fighting, a practitioner can employ the "*qi* and magnetic field" to detect and learn the opponent's changes. At this stage, listening energy is like a detector or probe that enables the practitioner to accurately collect the signals of strength, distance, direction, and so on given by the opponent. It means that the practitioner has approached the most advanced realm in which "the opponent does not know me; I know the opponent" and does not spare the slightest signals.

B. INQUIRING ENERGY

Inquiring energy refers to a technique that is employed when a practitioner does not know the opponent's real intention or deployment of energy and wants to know whether there is a trap. The practitioner emits some amount of energy to probe the opponent. If inquiring energy is well used, the practitioner will be able to get twice the result with half the effort.

Inquiring energy is a method and also a comprehensive technique. When utilizing inquiring energy, the practitioner should be flexible, adaptable, and both courageous and resourceful, and he should be good at gaining the initiative and victory by using strategy and skill.

Palm technique is commonly employed when using inquiring energy, but inquiring energy can also be used in a passive position. The latter case is called reverse inquiring energy.

For instance, when one's wrist and arm are grasped or one's chest and abdomen are pushed by the opponent in push-hands or fighting, reverse inquiring energy can be used. Reverse inquiring energy is an advanced technique which can be gradually mastered by a practitioner who has first mastered inquiring energy. If reverse inquiring energy is used well, the practitioner will not only get himself out of danger, but also turn defeat into victory in fighting by combining reverse inquiring energy with other techniques.

In push-hands or fighting, when any side uses inquiring energy, the other side will certainly respond accordingly. Roughly speaking, there are three ways for inquiring and answering, as follows.

First way

When we use invisible energy and light hand techniques for inquiring energy, the opponent may neglect the inquiry as he does not feel threatened. Instead, he may remain calm and wait for our movement. In this case, we should continue to exert some power on the opponent to get his answer to our inquiring energy and then sense his reaction.

Second way

When we continue to exert invisible energy and seep into the opponent in order to destroy his balance, he has to yield and try to neutralize our inquiring energy to keep his body centered and upright if he feels uncomfortable. At this moment, we should change inquiring energy quickly into pressing and following energy and attack his central point to destroy his defense.

However, it is worth noticing that the practitioner's centered and upright position should be kept when employing pressing and following energy. If it is not kept, the practitioner is making himself vulnerable and the opponent may take advantage of it.

Third way

When we are using inquiring energy to probe an opponent and the opponent is resisting with his real force, we should withdraw our inquiring energy quickly from the opponent to make his balance lost or, in other words, we should "guide the opponent to enter into emptiness." At this moment, we should make a quick decision and take the opportunity to emit energy according to the opponent's movements. This way we will surely win.

It is crucial to control inquiring energy well while employing it in push-hands. Inquiring energy should be used in the right context. Any excessive use of inquiring energy will expose our intention and energy to the opponent.

The opponent will certainly take advantage of the information and set a trap for us. If we use inquiring energy deficiently, we can neither probe the opponent's situation nor get a real "echo."

In order to achieve the goal of inquiring energy, a practitioner should be brave enough to go deep into the tiger cave, but he should also be cautious.

Characteristics of inquiring energy

Method	Probing the opponent's situation by changing contact points
Application and tendency of the energy	From the external to the internal, from the light to the heavy, and then from the heavy to the light
Nature	Inquiring, detection, and induction
Function	Guiding the opponent to enter into emptiness; affecting the opponent's center of gravity

C. INCH ENERGY

It is called inch energy when energy is emitted suddenly from within a very short distance. Inch energy is very effective in fighting. Also, it is difficult to defend against and too fast for the opponent to dodge or even to react to as it is released suddenly from within merely inches. It is so powerful and threatening that it is a special technique to injure the Zang-organs. When the opponent is negligent of his defense, a practitioner, with explosive inch energy, can destroy the opponent's mind/intent, *qi*, and spirit and make him shocked.

Inch energy has different names in different martial arts schools in China, including "shaking energy," "shocking energy," "explosive energy," and "pointing energy." It is described, in Taijiquan circles, as "the energy that is applied to a single point; it penetrates the bones wherever it lands." It does not seem to be very harmful externally, but it shocks and penetrates the inner organs due to its transmission internally when it lands on a human body.

A person will feel flustered and nauseous if he is attacked by inch energy. As a result, he may lose his fighting capacity or, worse, may spit blood and die. Actually, inch energy is a technique in Taijiquan that causes internal injury by striking externally. The above effects upon people can be made by a palm, fist, or elbow.

In fighting, inch energy will make shock waves inside the body. The waves come back when blocked, like the echo in a valley, and they form a resonance effect which lasts a long time. If the opponent's chest or abdomen is struck by inch energy, the shock waves in the thoracic cavity and the abdominal cavity will cause a tremor which shocks the inner organs and will shock them again as the waves hit the backbone and come back. Specifically speaking, the opponent will feel discomfort in the heart, be in cardiac arrhythmia or tachyarrhythmia, if his heart is attacked by inch energy; he will feel sick, vomit, or even spit blood if his stomach is hit; and he will suffer from internal hemorrhage if he is hit on the liver. In the latter cases, the waves, echo, and resonance are so powerful that some of the vessels in the stomach and liver are shocked or broken.

The reason for the terrible effectiveness of inch energy is that it is emitted and used on a single point, rather than it being quick and powerful. In fact, the more penetrating inch energy is, the more effective it will be. Especially, if a practitioner strikes constantly, the shock waves become tsunami-like—as when the waves coming behind drive on the waves before them—and the consequences will be even more serious. To prevent injury, in ordinary practice inch energy should be used very cautiously and its power should be very controlled. In fact, it should not be applied to anyone unless one's own life is threatened.

Taiji push-hands is an antagonistic sport. Two kinds of energy—long energy and short energy—are employed in push-hands and fighting.

Long energy can pitch the opponent out or make him fall. Long energy, in general, will not hurt people internally, or seriously. It is one of the skills often adopted in push-hands. Short energy means that one side emits inch energy to attack his opponent. As sudden as lightning, it gives an internal shock to the opponent, destroys the opponent's confidence, and deprives him of their fighting capacity, though it does not throw him far away.

How, then, can a practitioner develop and use inch energy properly? He should watch, study carefully, and practice repeatedly in daily exercise. Specifically, the insubstantial and the substantial should be allocated distinctly; alternation should be well conducted between high and low speed; and the fist should not be made tight until the hand reaches the opponent's body. At the same time, the mind/intent should combine with qi, and qi with power; the hand should conform to the foot, the elbow to the knee, and the shoulder to the hip. Only when having integrated the three internal harmonies with the three external harmonies can a practitioner concentrate the mind/intent, *qi*, spirit, and power and emit inch energy on a single point. This is the way to give full play to the power of inch energy.

Why would someone fail to have the expected effect even though he knows the requirements and does the movements correctly? The answer is that his *gongfu* is still inadequate. He needs to work hard and will surely succeed. As the proverb goes: "Constant effort yields sure success."

When *gongfu* is well cultivated, the penetrating effect produced by inch energy will be greater. If tactic and techniques are well applied, a practitioner can use the weak to win against the strong, use four ounces to attack one thousand pounds, and gain a victory with ingenious skills.

Demonstration of inch energy

Movement 1: When *B* makes a step forward with his right foot and strikes *A*'s chest with his right fist, *A* blocks and neutralizes the fist with his left hand. (Figures 8.1a, b)

FIGURE 8.1A

FIGURE 8.1B

Movement 2: *A* then stretches his right hand out and clenches his fingers when they arrive at *B*'s body to hit *B* on the chest. (Figure 8.2)

FIGURE 8.2

Characteristics: Inch energy may injure internally through hitting externally.

Advice: All the target positions for an inch energy attack on the body are vital positions. Practitioners in an inch energy exercise should be very cautious, and the power of inch energy should be well controlled to prevent accidental injuries.

D. SILK-REELING ENERGY

Silk-reeling energy is a unique and scientific method in practicing Taiji push-hands. It is actually a kind of internal skill (*neigong*) which lies concealed in the body, enters the joints, runs through the meridians, and flows throughout the entire body.

There are many kinds of silk-reeling energy, including inward spiral and outward spiral, large spiral and small spiral, left spiral and right spiral, upward spiral and downward spiral, forward spiral and backward spiral, and major-direction spiral and oblique-direction spiral. Generally speaking, however, silk-reeling energy can be divided into two kinds: *shun* (going with) spiral and *ni* (going against) spiral.

When the little finger goes down and the thumb goes up, the resulting spiral is *shun* spiral; when the thumb goes down and the little finger goes up, the resulting spiral is *ni* spiral. Another way of looking at it is: when the elbow goes outward and the energy opens outward, the resulting spiral is *ni* spiral; when the elbow closes inward and the energy goes inward, the resulting spiral is *shun* spiral. Additionally, the body and legs also stretch out and draw back spirally and make circular movements in push-hands.

The stages of training and development to be experienced by practitioners in exercising silk-reeling energy are as follows: first, changing large circles into medium circles; second, changing medium circles into small circles; and, finally, changing small circles into invisible (smallest) circles. The profound spiral is invisible and formless, which enables usage along the lines of the saying: "The energy is emitted at one point; it penetrates the bones wherever it lands."

For instance, if someone strikes you with a cotton-wadded quilt of 2500 grams as the weapon, you will certainly not think of it as a threatening attack, but you will surely consider it a dangerous strike if the weapon is a hammer of the same weight instead. That means that when the area of application becomes smaller, the weight or force concentrates and becomes more powerful and penetrating. When you apply silk-reeling energy to a dot on the opponent's body in push-hands or fighting, you can pit a small force against a large one, a weak force against a strong one, and four ounces to deflect one thousand pounds.

Silk-reeling is a basic technique and one of the important techniques for exercising Taiji push-hands. It is shown as rotations everywhere if silk--reeling energy is employed in push-hands. Silk-reeling makes all the joints spiral like balls, including the eighteen major joints of the neck, chest, waist, abdomen, buttocks, shoulders, elbows, wrists, crotch, knees, and feet. The eighteen balls spiral in different directions simultaneously at various positions and, as a result, make the entire body a Taiji spheroid in which motion and stillness co-exist, collection and emission are exchanged with each other, the internal and the external are combined into one, the upper and the lower move in unison, and all parts of the body are integrated with each other.

A Taiji classic states: "Silk-reeling energy should be everywhere in the entire body. The inward spiral and the outward spiral are emitted with movements. The energy is emitted from the heart, enters the joints, and reaches the muscles and skin externally." The five Zang-organs are in the chest and abdomen; the meridians and collaterals originate from the five Zang-organs; the Heart (mind) acts as the king of the entire body; the abdomen is the resource of inner *qi*; the waist plays the role of the starter; the chest functions as the room for neutralization; the spine serves as the path of *qi* in the *du* meridian; and the limbs are regarded as the way for movements.

If a practitioner does not absorb at the *qihai* in push-hands, and the chest and abdomen do not open and close, *zhong qi* (the *qi* of Spleen and Stomach in the Middle Jiao, especially referring to the Spleen *qi*) will not arrive at the *dantian*, and it will be difficult for the meridians to link together with each other.

Externally, one should utilize the spiral of the backbone and the folding and neutralizing functions of the chest and abdomen to drive the shoulders, elbows, wrists, hips, knees, feet, and neck spiral to make the upper and lower body, from top to toe, move in unison, the body move up and down spirally, all parts move while one part moves, all parts spiral while one part spirals, and form eighteen spiraling rings.

Internally, one should take the Heart (mind) and spirit as the monarch, originate *qi* from the Kidneys, and release it from the *dantian*. *Qi* will run through the meridians and collaterals, enter the joints, approach the tips of the four limbs, and return to the *dantian* after running throughout the entire body.

It is important to keep *qi* in the *dantian*. A practitioner, relying on spiral movements and the integration of the entire body, may cultivate a grain of *hunyuan qi* and form a stream (not several streams) of extraordinary spiraling inner energy. It is thus clear that the internal and external spiral movements are essential and most important. (Figure 8.3)

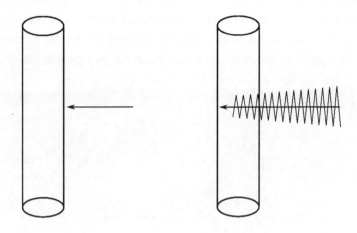

FIGURE 8.3 NON-SPIRAL FORCE IS NOT PENETRATING;
SPIRAL FORCE HAS A GREAT CAPACITY FOR PENETRATING

To understand the hows and whys behind the above and to use silk-reeling energy, a practitioner should exercise under the guidance of a qualified master, and after long-term practice, he will be able to master the *gongfu* of silk-reeling energy and improve his push-hands techniques.

Demonstration of silk-reeling

Movement 1: *B* makes a step forward with his right foot, grasps *A*'s two arms, and pushes forward. (Figure 8.4)

FIGURE 8.4

Movement 2: *A* keeps his right arm unmoved while spiraling his left arm and moving it backward to neutralize *B*'s push (*A* is utilizing smooth spiral and neutralizing energy). *A* keeps spiraling and neutralizing until *B*'s previous energy is spent and new energy has not yet generated. (Figure 8.5)

FIGURE 8.5

Movement 3: *A* moves quickly, spiraling with his left arm—which is a reverse spiral and uses a quick release of energy (*fajin*)—and pitches *B* out. At the same time his right arm helps in this. (Figure 8.6)

FIGURE 8.6

Characteristics: The energy spirals. It is applied to a single point and it penetrates the bones wherever it lands.

Advice: A pre-eminent Taijiquan master can technically reach the level at which "the opponent does not know me, but I know the opponent" in push-hands, because he makes spiral movements so that he can "vary his energy almost insensibly" and "vary his inner *qi* almost insensibly" through internal movements. He varies his paths, directions, and application points of energy to adapt to the opponent's movements and glue himself to the opponent's movements. However, his mind/intent and energy function just before the opponent's movements so that they are difficult for the opponent to discover.

The exercise of silk-reeling energy is so meticulous and advanced that silk-reeling energy has proved beneficial not only to health, but also to the development of technique.

E. EMITTING ENERGY

In appearance, emitting energy or quick release of energy (*fajin*) is done in various ways during push-hands, but actually all of them can be divided into two categories: long energy and short energy. The two are distinguished by the duration for which the energy is applied to the opponent's body.

Long energy originates from the feet, and it is controlled by the waist, transmitted through the spine, and utilized by the fingers, and so in this way, after going from the lower to the upper and threading up section by section, is emitted forward accordingly. A practitioner can often push the opponent far away without injuring him because of the long time in applying the energy.

Long energy is suitable for beginners who have not yet cultivated the sense of propriety in fighting. However, if a beginner emits long energy when he has not totally neutralized the opponent's energy, he will make the mistake of fighting force with force. The beginner will not win the admiration of the opponent even if he has struggled to push the opponent out.

The above mistake can be the result of any of the following three causes.

Cause 1

The beginner's obvious energy has not been totally removed, which makes it possible for the opponent to sense it and defend against it. The beginner fails to coordinate his three internal harmonies and three external harmonies and cannot combine the internal with the external or integrate all parts of the body so that he can only use an arm or a part of his body for emitting energy.

Cause 2

The quality of application of the technique of emitting energy depends upon whether the neutralizing energy is good and the intruding energy can be guided to enter into emptiness. When the opponent launches an attack, the beginner should use neutralizing energy to redirect the intruding energy and momentum first, and then emit energy as the opponent loses his balance and centered and upright status. This is the only way for the beginner to pitch the opponent out nimbly.

Cause 3

Some practitioners use the technique correctly, but they cannot get the desired results as they do not have adequate internal *gong*. Therefore, lack of power of internal *gong* is considered one of the causes of the bad emission of energy.

Short energy refers to inch energy, shock energy, or elbow technique employed to attack in push-hands. Owing to its short time, high speed, short distance, and integrated internal energy, short energy can create an extremely powerful penetrating and shocking force, which will make the opponent lose his adaptability and fighting ability.

In push-hands or martial applications, a practitioner should take the opponent's capacity into account and control, as carefully as possible, the length and strength of energy to be emitted in order to avoid injuries. Short energy is the internal emission of the energy of inner *gong*, so the exercise of inner *gong* lays the foundation of the emission of short energy. A practitioner should start the advanced exercise of short energy and its application when he has mastered long energy.

In the exercise of emitting short energy, efforts should be made to learn how to coordinate inhalation and exhalation.

Inhalation means to accumulate, which includes the accumulation of *qi* and energy. Inhalation also means to close, which includes closing in external movements and *qi*. During inhalation, the practitioner should make all the *qi*, energy, and movements properly closed and accumulated.

Exhalation means to open, to emit, or to release. If the practitioner has reached the advanced stage, accumulation and emission can be exchanged with each other whenever necessary. As the energy is so fast and powerful, and it lands so accurately, he emits suddenly at the contact point, which gives the opponent no time to react or neutralize before being pitched out. Do not hesitate to emit when the opportunity appears. A practitioner should be adaptable and decisive in taking actions.

A full inhalation and accumulation make a powerful and thorough emission. During inhalation, a practitioner should be able to lift the opponent's heels off the ground; during exhalation, a practitioner should be able to sink down and pitch the opponent out skillfully. While inhaling, *qi* is sunk to the *dantian*; while exhaling and emitting, *qi* arrives with the movements.

In daily exercise, a practitioner may choose a solo exercise to practice several energy-emitting movements. He may practice repeatedly the accumulation and emission forward, sideward, and backward, and create elastic and shaking energy in the arms, shoulders, chest, abdomen, hips, back, buttocks, and so on. He may then do exercises for two, where both sides "serve" or "feed" energy mutually and study together the proper extent of the accumulation and emission.

Demonstration of emitting energy

Movement 1: *B* makes a step forward and pushes *A*'s chest. (Figure 8.7)

FIGURE 8.7

Movement 2: At the very moment when *B*'s hands touch *A*'s chest, *A* "emits at a touch" and throws *B* out. (Figures 8.8, 8.9)

FIGURE 8.8

FIGURE 8.9

Characteristics: "Accumulate energy like drawing a bow; emit energy like shooting an arrow"; "emit at a touch"; and the energy is elastic, shaking, and explosive.

Advice: The above is an example of "emit at a touch," which shows a high standard of the exercise of the emission of energy. Exercises for promoting the quality of emitting energy include the following three steps:

1. "Guide the opponent's power to enter into emptiness, then immediately attack."

2. Emit when neutralizing, which means that neutralization exists in emission, whereas emission exists in neutralization.

3. "Emit at a touch."

F. NEUTRALIZING ENERGY

A practitioner will be able to develop his technique more effectively if he combines the exercises of neutralizing energy with emitting energy in practice, which actually means combining "guiding the opponent's energy to enter into emptiness" with "immediately attacking after neutralization." Completing only the exercise of neutralization without doing the emission exercise is considered getting only half-way. It may leave the opportunity for the opponent to change a passive situation into initiative. Therefore, we should follow the ancients' experience of "guiding the opponent's energy to enter into emptiness and then immediately attacking."

The process of the exercise of neutralizing energy is divided into three steps, as follows.

Step 1: "Guide first, then emit"

"Guide first, then emit" is the way to guide and neutralize the intruding energy, to make it enter into emptiness, and then to attack. Also, it is the stage of the primary exercise pursuing "large guiding and large attack." A lot of time should be spent mastering the soft and neutralizing energy of "giving up oneself and following the opponent." Exercises of "half guide and half attack" can then be started.

Step 2: "Half guide and half attack"

"Half guide and half attack" is the method in which some part of a practitioner's body moves backward a bit to "guide the opponent to enter into emptiness" and then "immediately attack." This is an exercise method for further training on neutralization after the technique of Step 1 has been mastered.

Step 3: "Attack when guiding"

"Attack when guiding" includes spiral movements, both internal and external. After completing the exercise of this step, movements of both sides will be more and more compact; the circles made by both sides will be smaller and smaller as skill progresses with practice. Practitioners develop the capacity to make their external movements and the changes of internal energy difficult to be sensed.

This technique may have various effects. For example, a practitioner seems to have hands everywhere on his body, neutralizes wherever is being touched, and attacks wherever is being touched; emission exists in neutralization, whereas neutralization exists in emission; and a practitioner rotates at a touch with a Taiji spheroid appearing wherever there is motion on his body.

Demonstration of neutralizing energy

Movements: When *B*, with his right hand, pushes *A* forcefully at the left part of the chest, *A* rotates leftward from the waist to neutralize the attack. At the same time, *A*, with his right hand, pushes *B* at the left part of the chest until *B* is guided to enter into emptiness or loses balance. (Figures 8.10–8.12)

FIGURE 8.10

FIGURE 8.11

FIGURE 8.12

Characteristics: Soft or hard. Never separate or resist. Give up oneself and follow the opponent. Guide the opponent to enter into emptiness.

Advice: The neutralizing energy shown in this movement is just like revolving doors when they rotate, and complete neutralization and emission at the same time when they are pushed.

G. CUTTING ENERGY

Movements: *B* steps forward with his right foot and, with his right fist, punches *A* at the chest. *A* grabs *B*'s right wrist with his left hand and pushes it down, and then holds *B*'s right elbow with his right hand, twisting it upward to bend the joint backward in order to cut in *B*'s attack. (Figures 8.13–8.15)

FIGURE 8.13

FIGURE 8.14

FIGURE 8.15

Characteristics: This technique is quite efficient in fighting as it cuts off the opponent's energy and "controls the opponent by a late attack."

Advice: Cutting energy enables a practitioner, at the very beginning of a match, to control any one of the opponent's nine kinds of main joint: shoulders, elbows, hands, hips, knees, feet, neck, spine, and lower back. Furthermore, it has the functions of injuring the opponent's muscles, misplacing his bones at joints, and intercepting his energy and *qi*.

There are many kinds of methods for using cutting energy in push-hands and fighting, including splitting energy, seizing, and joint-locking, and counter-techniques to seizing and joint-locking. In exercise, a practitioner should attach vital importance to the opportune moment. If the practitioner employs cutting energy too early, the opponent has not emitted his energy yet, and if cutting energy is employed later than it should be and the opponent is more powerful and technically skillful, the practitioner will find himself in a passive situation.

H. CROSSING ENERGY (DEFLECTING ONE THOUSAND POUNDS WITH FOUR OUNCES)

Movements: *B* grasps *A*'s collar tightly with his right hand. *A* responds by locking *B*'s right hand with his right hand and pushes his left hand on *B*'s right elbow. Then *A* moves from left to right, simultaneously pivoting at the waist, and lowers his center of gravity to "deflect" *B* to fall to the ground. (Figures 8.16–8.18)

FIGURE 8.16

FIGURE 8.17

FIGURE 8.18

Characteristics: The practitioner can defeat powerful, straight intruding energy by technical utilization of crossing energy.

Advice: Crossing energy means a technique to defeat powerful, straight intruding energy by usage of crossing energy. The utilization of crossing energy keeps the opponent from bringing his *gongfu*, energy, and techniques into normal play. In employing crossing energy to deal with an intruding force, the shorter the distance or the shorter the moment of force is, the greater the crossing energy needs to be, and the lesser the crossing energy will affect. In contrast, the longer the distance or the moment of force is, the smaller the crossing energy needs to be, and the better it will affect. This is the technique of "deflecting one thousand pounds with four ounces." (Figure 8.19)

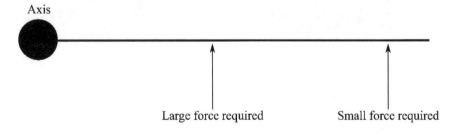

FIGURE 8.19 THE AMOUNT OF CROSSING ENERGY REQUIRED
DEPENDS ON THE DISTANCE TO THE AXIS

How, then, to "deflect one thousand pounds with four ounces" when a force of a thousand pounds is applied to your body or when your force is meeting the opponent's force? First of all, you must have the capacity to bear the force of one thousand pounds; then you should employ techniques unique to Taiji push-hands, such as "giving up yourself and following the opponent," "guiding the opponent's energy to enter into emptiness," and "borrowing the opponent's energy to strike the opponent," to have the effect of using a small force to defeat a great force, and using ingenuity to win victory, which means to "deflect one thousand pounds with four ounces."

If a practitioner is not backed by the capacity of bearing a force as powerful as one thousand pounds, the technique of "deflecting one thousand pounds with four ounces" will be only a dream. This is why some people cannot acquire the desired results whenever they are doing push-hands, though they have understood the hows and whys and made the movements correctly.

One's actual strength (*gongfu*) should not be neglected, but, in push-hands and fighting, it is emphasized that people should employ skills to defeat their opponents rather than, like the external school of martial arts, "employ a great force to fight a small one," "use the strong to beat the weak," or "pit one thousand pounds against one thousand pounds."

I. DANTIAN ENERGY

Movements: *B* steps out and pushes *A* on the *dantian* area with both his hands. *A* mobilizes the internal *qi* of his *dantian* to pitch *B* out with a wave of the *dantian qi*. (Figures 8.20, 8.21)

FIGURE 8.20

FIGURE 8.21

Characteristics: *Dantian* takes shape; internal *qi* rotates and surges forward and backward.

Advice: If a practitioner has cultivated a lot of internal *qi*, like a ball filled with gas, at the middle *dantian*, he will be able to use his *dantian qi* to pitch the opponent out or use his *dantian* to seize the opponent.

J. SPRING ENERGY (MOVING DOWN BEFORE MOVING UP)

Movements: As *B* holds both of *A*'s forearms and tries to press them down, *A* lowers his arms following *B*'s movements to "guide the opponent's energy to enter into emptiness." When *B*'s energy is spent and new energy has not yet generated, *A* springs his arms upward, pitching *B* out. (Figures 8.22–8.24)

FIGURE 8.22

FIGURE 8.23

FIGURE 8.24

Characteristics: The accumulation of energy is like pressing a spring, whereas the rebound is like a bullet being shot.

Advice: This is an example where the practitioner employs the technique of "moving down before moving up" to spring and pitch the opponent out in Taiji push-hands. (Figure 8.25)

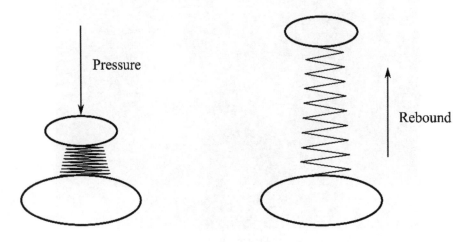

FIGURE 8.25 THE BUILD-UP AND RELEASE OF SPRING ENERGY

To learn and practice Taiji push-hands and fighting art, a practitioner needs to learn to put some mechanical formula into the practice of push-hands. However, the practitioner should keep in his mind that he should act according to circumstances all the time, though the mechanical formulae are never changed. Therefore, emphasis should be put on combining theory with practice in push-hands and fighting.

K. ALTERNATING BETWEEN YIN AND YANG (MOVING RIGHT BEFORE MOVING LEFT)

Movements: *B* holds and pushes *A*'s arms forcefully. *A*, with his left arm, exerts some force from left to right. When *B* bears the force, *A* changes his left arm from substantial into insubstantial, guiding *B*'s energy to enter into emptiness. *A* keeps the right arm substantial and moves it forward, which is to "immediately attack." Simultaneously, *A* pivots leftward at the waist to coordinate with his arms in "alternating between yin and yang." (Figures 8.26–8.28)

FIGURE 8.26

FIGURE 8.27

FIGURE 8.28

Characteristics: Yin dwells in yang, and yang dwells in yin; yin and yang coordinate mutually; and they act just like the Taiji symbol shows.

Advice: *A*, with his left arm, exerts some force from left to right in order to make *B* misjudge his intention. *A* suddenly changes his left arm into an insubstantial one like when he removes *B*'s crutch. This is an example of the practitioner utilizing the method of "moving rightward before moving leftward" to "alternate between yin and yang" in push-hands.

L. GUIDING THE OPPONENT'S ENERGY TO ENTER INTO EMPTINESS (TO MOVE BACKWARD BEFORE MOVING FORWARD)

Movements: *B* holds *A*'s arms and pushes them with force. *A* moves his left arm backward following *B*'s movement to guide *B*'s energy to enter into emptiness. As *B*'s old energy has passed and his next energy has not been created yet, *A* moves his arms forward quickly and emits energy to pitch *B* out. (Figures 8.29–8.31)

FIGURE 8.29

FIGURE 8.30

FIGURE 8.31

Characteristics: Giving up oneself and following the opponent; leading the opponent's energy like diverting and discharging the flood; and guiding the opponent's energy to enter into emptiness and then attacking immediately.

Advice: The training method of "moving backward before moving forward" is employed in practice to "guide the opponent's energy to enter into emptiness" based on the principle of acting force and counteracting force. In the exercise employing the technique of "guiding the opponent's energy to enter into emptiness," one's movements and energy should perfectly match those of the opponent without being early or late, faster or slower, or separating from the opponent. This is an example where the practitioner employs the method of "moving backward before moving forward" to "guide the opponent's energy to enter into emptiness and immediately attack" in Taiji push-hands.

To "guide the opponent's energy to enter into emptiness and immediately attack," a practitioner should experience the following three phases.

Phase 1: *Guiding the opponent and his energy in*
The practitioner should be brave enough to allow the opponent to come up close to him and let the opponent's energy get into him.

Phase 2: *Making the opponent and his energy enter into emptiness*
After Phase 1, the practitioner makes the opponent and his energy enter into emptiness by making various rotations or alternating between yin and yang.

Phase 3: *Attacking immediately*
When the opponent has tilted and lost balance because he or his energy was guided to enter into emptiness, the practitioner should emit energy quickly until the opponent is pitched out.

M. OPENING–CLOSING ENERGY

Movements: *B* makes a step forward with his right foot, holds *A*'s arms, and pushes them forcefully. *A* opens his arms to neutralize the intruding energy and then closes his arms, combines his mind/intent with his movements, and emits energy toward the center of *B*'s body to pitch *B* out. (Figures 8.32, 8.33)

FIGURE 8.32

FIGURE 8.33

Characteristics: Closing exists in opening; opening exists in closing; and opening and closing change into each other.

Advice: The opening movement is to "guide the opponent and his energy to enter into emptiness," and then the closing movement means to "immediately attack."

N. FOLDING ENERGY

Movements: *B* strikes *A* on the chest with his right palm. As *B*'s palm just approaches *A*'s chest, *A* leans forward and seizes *B*'s palm with his chest. (Figures 8.34, 8.35)

FIGURE 8.34

FIGURE 8.35

Characteristics: The chest and abdomen open and close; seizing is done by folding energy.

Advice: The folding energy applied in Taiji push-hands is cultivated through the exercise named "folding with chest and abdomen." Folding energy is emphasized in Taiji classics and often used for seizing and joint-locking with the chest or abdomen. The energy is special, as one's chest acts like a revolving trap-plate when it is struck by the opponent's palm. The revolving trap-plate pivots on a central axis. If the lower part is pushed backward by the opponent's energy, the upper will move down and forward. The more powerful the opponent's intruding energy is, the more powerful the returning energy is. Thus, the seizing and joint-locking is completed and the opponent is attacked through folding with the chest and abdomen. (Figure 8.36)

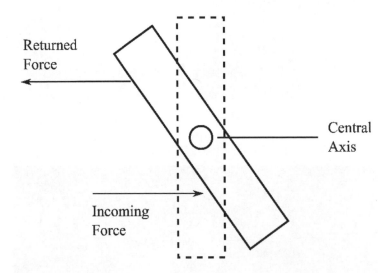

FIGURE 8.36 FOLDING ENERGY WORKS LIKE A REVOLVING TRAP-PLATE

Another example: If you attack the opponent with the palm, the palm should be able to rotate like a revolving trap-plate and pivot on the wrist. When the palm approaches the opponent, it rotates accordingly so that you can control the opponent's energy and put him in a passive position.

O. DEFLECTING THE TIP SECTION

Movements: *B* steps forward with his right foot and strikes *A* on the chest with his right fist. *A*, with his left hand, deflects *B*'s right fist, makes *A* step forward with his right foot, and pushes *B*'s forehead when his right leg has been positioned against the back of *B*'s right leg to make *B* fall. (Figures 8.37–8.40)

FIGURE 8.37

FIGURE 8.38

FIGURE 8.39

FIGURE 8.40

Characteristics: Deflect the tip section and cut the root section.

Advice: In Taiji push-hands, it is instinctive to pit the strong against the weak. However, it is the specialty of Taijiquan to pit the weak against the strong and gain victory by fighting the opponent skillfully. (Figure 8.41)

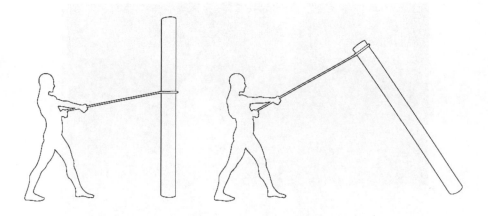

FIGURE 8.41 EXAMPLE OF PULLING A WOODEN STAKE

P. SHOVELING THE ROOT SECTION

Movements: *B* steps out, holds *A*'s arms, and pushes him forcefully. *A* puts the palms side by side like a shovel and aims at *B*'s heels until *B* is shoveled out. (Figures 8.42–8.44)

FIGURE 8.42

FIGURE 8.43

FIGURE 8.44

Characteristics: Stay clear of the opponent's main force and strike on his weak points; maximize your strong points and avoid using your weak points.

Advice: Shoveling the root section is one of the techniques for staying away from the opponent's main force and striking him on his weak points. To utilize the technique, you should pinpoint the opponent's resources of energy before setting your target. This technique can also be applied to the hips, abdomen, chest, arms, and others. (Figure 8.45)

FIGURE 8.45 SHOVELING THE ROOT SECTION

Q. SHIFTING ENERGY

Movement 1: *B* steps out and pushes *A*'s chest fiercely with his palms. *A* neutralizes *B*'s attack with the technique of warding off. (Figures 8.46, 8.47)

FIGURE 8.46

FIGURE 8.47

Movement 2: *A* then pushes *B*'s chest with his hands so that the substantial and the insubstantial, and the hardness and softness, exchange constantly between the force points on *A*'s hands. When *B* moves backward, *A* steps forward to follow him. (Figures 8.48, 8.49)

FIGURE 8.48

FIGURE 8.49

Characteristics: The substantial and the insubstantial alternate; the hardness and softness compensate each other; and the force points change their positions.

Advice: Understanding energy should be learnt in the following dimensions.

Dimension 1: Strategy

One should learn how to "know himself as well as the opponent" and "pit one's strong points against the opponent's weak points."

Dimension 2: Tactics

One should learn how to employ the unique Taiji techniques to attack or defend.

Dimension 3: Torso and limbs

When some part of a practitioner's body is attacked, he should learn how to destroy the opponent's attack.

Dimension 4: Movements

As the proverb goes: "There is no square without ruler and there is no circle without compasses"; the practitioner should exercise the concerned movements and techniques. Gradually, he will approach the level at which he can go beyond rules and, at the same time, in line with the rules, do everything desired.

Dimension 5: Footwork

One should learn how to employ agile and adaptable footwork to launch a roundabout attack after the front attack has proved impossible.

Dimension 6: Bodywork

One should learn how to adjust his body to maintain its "centered and upright" state without tilting, relying on his bodywork and footwork.

Dimension 7: Energy

One should learn how to employ various Taiji energies in push-hands or fighting.

Dimension 8: Internal gong

One should learn how to use his internal *gong* in various movements of push-hands or martial applications.

R. RELAXING–SINKING ENERGY

Movement 1: *B* steps out and pushes *A*'s arms forcefully. *A* uses silk-reeling energy to neutralize *B*'s attack. (Figures 8.50, 8.51)

FIGURE 8.50

FIGURE 8.51

Movement 2: *A* then conforms to *B*'s movements and puts his arms on *B*'s arms or shoulders and leans his upper chest against *B*'s body. *A* wraps, covers, presses, and binds *B*'s body with a large net made up of his spirit, mind/intent, internal *qi*, and body. (Figures 8.52, 8.53)

FIGURE 8.52

FIGURE 8.53

Movement 3: *A* varies according to *B*'s changes of movements. In this situation, there are a lot of ways for *A* to attack *B*.

Characteristics: The softness can be used to conquer the hardness. A needle is covered by cotton.

Advice: Relaxing–sinking energy is a technical method for exercising the "Four-Word Secret" mentioned in Taiji classics. Movements of relaxing–sinking energy seem to be formless and indefinite. The Four-Word Secret is so profound that only well-cultivated internal *gong* may enable a practitioner to understand its deep meaning.

The Four-Word Secret includes:

- *Coating*: Coating refers to the technique of conducting your *qi* in your own body and coating the opponent's energy to make it impossible for him to move.

- *Covering*: Covering refers to the technique of using your *qi* to cover the position where the opponent comes.

- *Targeting*: Targeting refers to the technique of releasing your *qi* aiming at the position where the opponent comes.

- *Swallowing*: Swallowing refers to the technique of using your *qi* to swallow the entire opponent and enter into a situation of neutralization.

S. THREE-SECTION ENERGY

Movement 1: *B* steps out and attacks *A* with a blow to the chest. *A* deflects and neutralizes the opponent's right fist, and simultaneously returns a chin blow to *B* with his right fist. (Figures 8.54, 8.55)

FIGURE 8.54

FIGURE 8.55

Movement 2: In the event that *A* fails in his fist strike, he may change to use his right elbow to strike *B* on the chest. (Figure 8.56)

FIGURE 8.56

Movement 3: In the event that *A*'s elbow blow is also not effective, *A* may change and strike *B* with his right shoulder until *B* is shouldered out. (Figure 8.57)

FIGURE 8.57

Characteristics: "Punching at a distance, elbowing when getting nearer and shouldering when pressing close to the opponent" empower a practitioner to break through the opponent's three lines of defense.

Advice: Three-section energy is an attacking technique which is used by one who masters a high standard in Taiji push-hands and fighting technique, and is able to adapt to changing conditions and do whatever he desires. As a Taiji proverb goes: "The attack with three-section energy arrives invisibly. It is not considered skillful to make visible attacks."

T. REMOTE ENERGY

Movements: When *A* attacks *B* with his palm, he imagines that he is throwing a "*qi* ball" at the opponent and the ball will explode when it hits the opponent on the body. (Figure 8.58)

FIGURE 8.58 QI BALL OF REMOTE ENERGY HITTING THE OPPONENT

Characteristics: The external *dan* is globular and, launched by energy, it explodes when it hits the target.

Advice: At the advanced stage, some technical movements will be completed by multiple energies instead of a single kind of energy. Furthermore, the movements are supported by internal *gong* which creates the situation of "when the mind/intent arrives, *qi* arrives; when *qi* arrives, force arrives." In this case, energy is difficult to express simply with dynamic formulae. One should be able to experience that the *qi* ball is emitted when energy is emitted by a palm or a fist, but only when one's internal *gong* has reached the stage of external *dan gong*.

U. SUMMARY

In summary, Taijiquan is a sport of mind and *qi*. Exercising of Taiji push-hands is actually a process to coordinate the movements and *qi*. The movements are methods, whereas *qi* is the content. One will be able to acquire a merely elementary effect if he staggers at the phase of visible movements. He will reach an advanced stage marked by the "combination of mind/intent, *qi*, and movements" and really master the principle of movements of Taiji push-hands only when he has greatly promoted his level of *qi* of internal *gong*.

— CHAPTER IX —

Seizing and Joint-Locking Techniques and Counter-Techniques

Seizing and joint-locking (*qinna*) techniques and counter-techniques refer to a system of fighting techniques used at close quarters. This chapter introduces techniques of the system with various kinds of attacks.

A. SEIZING AND JOINT-LOCKING TECHNIQUES

1. Using the hands

Movements: *B* makes a step forward with his right foot and tries to strike *A* on the chest with his right palm. *A* locks *B*'s right wrist with his left hand and pulls it backward and, at the same time, pushes *B*'s fingers forward to perform a joint-locking technique. (Figures 9.1–9.3)

Figure 9.1

Figure 9.2

Figure 9.3

2. Using the elbow

Movements: *B* makes a step forward with his left foot and tries to strike *A* on the chest with his left fist. *A* grasps *B*'s left wrist with his left hand, steps out, and puts his right elbow on *B*'s left elbow. When *A* gains control of *B*'s elbow joint, he suddenly lifts *B*'s left hand up and, at the same time, presses *B*'s right elbow down. (Figures 9.4–9.6)

FIGURE 9.4

FIGURE 9.5

FIGURE 9.6

3. Using the shoulder

Movements: *B* steps out and, with his left fist, attempts to strike *A* on the chest. *A* first deflects the strike with his left hand and seizes *B*'s left fist with both hands. *A* then advances following *B*'s movements; he turns and puts *B*'s left elbow on his (*A*'s) shoulder. When *B*'s elbow is under control, *A* suddenly pulls *B*'s left fist down and, at the same time, pushes upward with his shoulders. (Figures 9.7–9.9)

FIGURE 9.7

FIGURE 9.8

FIGURE 9.9

4. Using the chest

Movements: *B* makes a step forward with his right foot and strikes *A* on the chest with his right palm. *A* grasps *B*'s right wrist with his right hand and closes the left part of his chest downward to lock *B*'s right hand. (Figures 9.10–9.12)

FIGURE 9.10

FIGURE 9.11

FIGURE 9.12

5. *Using the dantian*

Movements: *B* makes a step forward with his right foot and strikes *A* on the abdomen with his right palm. *A* grasps *B*'s right wrist, rotates the *dantian* "ball" to "guide *B*'s energy to enter into emptiness," and locks *B*'s right hand. (Figures 9.13–9.15)

FIGURE 9.13

FIGURE 9.14

FIGURE 9.15

B. SEIZING AND JOINT-LOCKING COUNTER-TECHNIQUES

1. Counter-technique with the hands

Movements: *B* makes a step forward with his right foot and grasps *A*'s right wrist with his right hand. *A* grasps and presses *B*'s right hand with his left hand and makes a silk-reeling spiral with his right hand to perform a counter-technique. (Figures 9.16–9.18)

FIGURE 9.16

FIGURE 9.17

FIGURE 9.18

2. Counter-technique with the elbow

Movements: *B* makes a step forward with his right foot, grasps *A*'s right wrist with his right hand, and holds *A*'s right elbow with his left hand. *A* makes a circle with his right elbow and, at the same time, grasps *B*'s right hand and presses *B*'s arm down with his right elbow, forming a counter-hold. (Figures 9.19–9.21)

FIGURE 9.19

FIGURE 9.20

FIGURE 9.21

3. Countering with silk-reeling

Movements: *B* makes a step forward with his right foot, grasps *A*'s left arm with his right hand, and holds *A*'s right elbow with his left hand. *A* makes a counterclockwise circle with his left arm to neutralize *B*'s force and advances to deliver a shoulder blow against *B* to knock him away. (Figures 9.22–9.24)

FIGURE 9.22

FIGURE 9.23

FIGURE 9.24

4. Countering a front bear hug

Movements: *B* wraps his arms around *A* from the front. To counter *B*'s hold, *A* puts his left hand on top of *B*'s head and his right hand on *B*'s chin, and then twists *B*'s head. (Figures 9.25–9.27)

FIGURE 9.25

FIGURE 9.26

FIGURE 9.27

5. Countering a rear bear hug

Movements: *B* wraps his arms around *A* from the rear. *A* quickly bends forward, grips and forcefully lifts one of *B*'s legs up, and, at the same time, assumes a sitting position to use his body weight to press the upper end of *B*'s thigh downward to make *B* fall to the ground. (Figures 9.28–9.30)

FIGURE 9.28

FIGURE 9.29

FIGURE 9.30

CHAPTER X

Leg Techniques

A. HEEL KICK

Movements: *B* steps out with his left foot and delivers a straight blow, using his left hand, towards *A*. *A* neutralizes *B*'s attack with his right hand and kicks *B* in the left ribs with his right heel. (Figures 10.1–10.3)

FIGURE 10.1   FIGURE 10.2

FIGURE 10.3

B. TOE KICK

Movements: *B* steps out with his right foot and aims a straight blow at *A* with his right hand. *A* neutralizes *B*'s attack by using his left hand to push *B*'s punching hand down. After that, he kicks *B*'s chin with his right foot and strikes the top of *B*'s head with his right palm. (Figures 10.4–10.6)

FIGURE 10.4

FIGURE 10.5

FIGURE 10.6

C. LOTUS KICK

Movements: *B* steps forward with his right foot and aims a straight punch at *A*. *A* uses his right hand to parry *B*'s punch, advances to close in upon *B*, places his right leg against the hollow of *B*'s right knee, and brings his right palm on *B*'s neck. *A* then simultaneously kicks backward and, with the right palm on *B*'s neck, chops forward. (Figures 10.7–10.10)

FIGURE 10.7

FIGURE 10.8

FIGURE 10.9

FIGURE 10.10

D. FOOT SICKLE (PULLING FOOT SWEEP)

Movements: *B* steps out with his left foot and delivers a straight blow, using his left hand, towards *A*. *A* neutralizes *B*'s punch by pushing *B*'s fist down; he advances and puts his right foot behind *B*'s left foot. *A* then pulls his right foot towards himself and away from *B* while hooking *B*'s left foot to make *B* lose his balance and fall. (Figures 10.11–10.13)

FIGURE 10.11

FIGURE 10.12

FIGURE 10.13

E. DOUBLE KICK (MANDARIN DUCK KICK)

Movements: *B* kicks *A* with his right foot. With his left leg, *A* first kicks *B*'s right leg to block and neutralize the attack, and then takes the opportunity to kick *B* at the left knee joint with the heel of his left foot. (Figures 10.14–10.16)

FIGURE 10.14

FIGURE 10.15

FIGURE 10.16

F. SWEEPING LEG

Movements: *B* steps out with his left foot and delivers a straight blow, using his left hand, towards *A*. *A* parries and neutralizes *B*'s left fist with his left hand and, at the same time, sweeps *B*'s left leg with his right leg. (Figures 10.17–10.19)

FIGURE 10.17

FIGURE 10.18

FIGURE 10.19

G. STANDING ON ONE LEG

Movements: *B* steps forward with his right foot and tries to punch *A* with his right hand. *A* pushes *B*'s right fist downwards to neutralize the attack. *A* then thrusts his right knee into *B*'s lower abdomen and, at the same time, strikes *B*'s chin with his right fist. (Figures 10.20–10.22)

FIGURE 10.20

FIGURE 10.21

FIGURE 10.22

CHAPTER XI

Vital Point Striking

Vital point striking originated from the Taoist Inner Dan Gong in ancient times in China. It is to strike the opponent's acupuncture points in the blink of an eye and make the meridians suddenly shut, the inner *qi* blocked, the points blunt, functions of a part or the entire body impaired, and defense capacity lost.

Vital point striking has developed along with the rise of the Chinese martial arts and Chinese traditional medicine, and it has been integrated with the fighting techniques of Wushu and the Tuina of Chinese traditional medicine. It can be used to destroy an opponent if it is used in combat or to save a life if used medically.

Since ancient times, point striking has been used and developed in two parallel ways. When it is used for therapy, its effects are obvious. However, its second use, in fighting, is seldom witnessed. The reason is that there are only a few people who have the opportunity to learn the skill of point striking. In fact, all masters, regardless of their Wushu school, share the same rule: "Rather go without than have a gangster [people without good virtue and behavior] heir."

A master is extremely restricted and cautious in choosing an heir to the skill of point striking among his formally registered disciples. Only if a disciple is considered eligible in both virtue and technique can he be taught the skill. That is why very few people really understand vital point striking. The skill, as a rarely taught secret technique, has long been shrouded in a dense fog of mystery.

A. IMMEDIATE RESULTS AND CONCEALED RESULTS

What is point striking then? *Secret of Wudang* states: "To shut the vital communication paths (inside of the opponent's body), to cut his transmission, to make him dizzy when the strike is not powerful or die when powerful."

There are a lot of meridians and collaterals which serve as the conduits of *qi* and blood, the system for coordinating the entire body internally, and the system for connecting the internal and the external. The acupuncture points on the meridians and collaterals are vital to the living activities of a human being as they are closely related to thinking and the ability to act. This explanation of life has been proven true during the many centuries' practice of Chinese traditional medicine and it has also laid the foundational theory for vital point striking:

- *Immediate results*: When most important points (or some vital positions) are struck, immediate results are obtained. Some functions are seriously impaired in the concerned area or even in the entire body, including the loss of *qi*, intolerable pain, difficulty in breathing, and disabled movements. Every symptom will be removed instantly when a relief therapy is completed.

- *Concealed results*: When the important points are struck, the lesions will be longstanding in general or manifest gradually or become serious after a period of time. This is called "inner injury" by people in Wushu society.

According to point-striking theory, the result varies according to which different points have been struck with different hand techniques. Points are classified as the following: *qi*-stagnancy-connected points, numbness-connected points, palsy-connected points, dumbness-connected points, death-connected points, and body-fixation-connected points. There are 36 points named 36 VIP (very important points).

It remains a mystery how point striking functions—a mystery of not only Wushu, but also medicine, ergonomics, and life. It poses a question for study. If the techniques and effects could be verified by methods of modern science, maybe human beings' physique and health situation could be benefited greatly.

B. OPERATING METHOD OF POINT STRIKING

Point-striking practitioners spare no effort to improve their striking strength and accuracy in locating the points. The training methods recommended here come from materials handed down generation by generation from the ancients.

For instance, the silk-reeling and twisting methods in the Taiji Stick and Ruler exercise are designed for training the palms and fingers. After long-term exercise, a practitioner can concentrate all his power on one point and make the power penetrate the bones. Also, practitioners exercise Jingang (Buddha's warrior attendant) Finger Gong to promote the strength of the strike against a point and the accuracy of attacking. In order to accurately strike target points, one should be very familiar with the meridians and collaterals and exercise repeatedly. In ancient times, practitioners created training tools, such as wooden and bronze models, to practice and master point striking.

C. POINT STRIKING ACCORDING TO TIME OF DAY

One of the technical characteristics of vital point striking is that it is utilized according to the time of day. A strike may obtain great results when it is carried out against a point at a relevant time.

According to a proverb: "Striking a person on a minor point causes injury; striking a person on a vital one causes death." This proverb originates from the theory of Midday–Midnight Point Selection (Zi Wu Liu Zhu) in Chinese traditional medicine. It refers to the belief that *qi* and blood run along the twelve meridians and collaterals, and the running situation varies in the twelve different time periods (double hours) of a day and changes periodically. It is believed that, during a certain span of two hours, *qi* and blood are especially vigorous along a specific meridian or collateral and at one or more points on the meridian or collateral.

Therefore, the theory of point striking according to time explains that the flow of *qi* and blood will be stopped, the transportation throughout the body cut off, and functions impaired if a point where *qi* and blood are especially vigorous is struck. Some precious materials handed down from ancient times list points selected for each two-hour period with accompanying explanations (materials including the *Graphic Representation of Thirty-six Very Important Points, Graphic Representation of Target Points at 1–3 O'clock in the Morning,* and *Graphic Representation of Target Points at 3–5 O'clock in the Morning*).

1. Secrets of point striking related to flow of qi and blood

Qi and blood throughout the body have a head, it runs day and night.

If a man is hit at the right time and the right point, seven days later the man will die.

At 1–3 o'clock find it at Jingquan, it goes to the heart at midnight.

Shangen is the point at 5–7 after Jingkou 3–5, it arrives at Fengtou at 9–11 after Tianxin 7–9.

It visits Zhongyuan midday, during 13–15 it is with two Changong, left and right.

Fengwei is connected with 15–17 and Qujing 17–19, 19–21 is Danshen's time.

Liugong should wait for 21–23, don't tell a criminal.

2. Timetable for point striking

Gallbladder Channel is flourishing	at 23–1 o'clock
Liver Channel is flourishing	at 1–3 o'clock
Lung Channel is flourishing	at 3–5 o'clock
Large Intestine Channel is flourishing	at 5–7 o'clock
Stomach Channel is flourishing	at 7–9 o'clock
Spleen Channel is flourishing	at 9–11 o'clock
Heart Channel is flourishing	at 11–13 o'clock
Small Intestine Channel is flourishing	at 13–15 o'clock
Bladder Channel is flourishing	at 15–17 o'clock
Kidney Channel is flourishing	at 17–19 o'clock
Pericardium Channel is flourishing	at 19–21 o'clock
Sanjiao Channel is flourishing	at 21–23 o'clock

Qi and blood flow to the Gallbladder at 23–1 o'clock

The Gallbladder acts as a judicial judge, and it is where the decisions are made and issued. It pertains to Wood in the five elements and is attached to the Liver. It is also named Zhong Jing Zhi Fu (the organ of middle essence). All eleven collaterals are dominated by the Gallbladder. It is the Gallbladder which makes a human being brave or timid, and honest or evil. Therefore, humans depend on the Gallbladder. A human being can take the responsibility for things in the world only if he has courage (a great capacity of the Gallbladder). The Gallbladder governs the goodness with which a human being is free from all anxieties. The Gallbladder is attached to the short part of the Liver. It belongs to the meridian of Foot-Shaoyang and has little blood and abundant *qi*.

Qi and blood flow to the Liver at 1–3 o'clock

The Liver acts as an official of a general, and it is where strategy comes from. It pertains to Wood in the five elements. As a Zang-organ, where the soul dwells, the Liver is located under the diaphragm. There are collaterals which connect the Liver with the lower part of the Pericardium. The Liver is attached to the Gallbladder. In Chinese, the Liver has the same pronunciation as a trunk, as it looks like a trunk with branches, which governs the tendons and presents on the hands. It opens into the eyes, belongs to the meridian of Foot-Jueyin, and has abundant blood and little *qi*.

Qi and blood flow to the Lung at 3–5 o'clock

The Lung has the capacity of a liaison official, and it is where the coordination of visceral activities comes from. The Lung pertains to Metal in the five elements. As a Zang-organ, where the spirit dwells, the Lung acts as the chief of the five Zang-organs, the cover of the Heart, and the origin of *qi*. Its upper part connects to the throat orifice and its lower part covers Zang-organs and controls inhalation and exhalation. It therefore nurtures and protects the entire body. The word Lung is derived from the word "abundant," as it has twenty-four orifices and distributes clean air and turbid air to various Zang-organs. The clean air and turbid air are so abundant that they are not preventable. It is internally–externally related with the skin and hair. It opens into the nose, belongs to the meridian of Taiyin, and has little blood and abundant *qi*.

Qi and blood flow to the Large Intestine at 5–7 o'clock

The Large Intestine serves as an official in charge of transmission, and it is where the five tastes come from. It pertains to Earth in the five elements. It is a Fu-organ attached to the Spleen, so it subordinates to the land. The land is for growing the five cereals, and the Large Intestine serves as the "market of the five cereals." In addition, the Stomach means technique and method. When the water and cereals enter into the Stomach, vital essence is produced. The essence travels upwards and gets discharged through the Lung, or it flows to the limbs and all over the body to protect a human being externally and strengthen him internally. The Large Intestine is located under the diaphragm and on the right side of the Small Intestine, connecting up to the throat. It belongs to the meridian of Foot-Yangming and has abundant blood and little *qi*.

Qi and blood flow to the Stomach at 7–9 o'clock

The Stomach is located in the Middle Jiao. It pertains to Earth in the five elements. In the *Ling Shu Yu Ban*, it reads: "The Stomach has some room in it and is able to receive and digest, improves the appetite for eating, and produces *qi* and blood. The Stomach is the sea of water, food, *qi*, and blood." In the *Su Wen Yu Ji Zhen Zang Lun*, it reads: "All the five Zang-organs get *qi* from the Stomach and depend on it. It is considered normal for the Stomach *qi* to descend."

Qi and blood flow to the Spleen at 9–11 o'clock

The Spleen, under the diaphragm, is situated in the Middle Jiao. It pertains to Earth in the five elements. It is considered as the extreme Yang among various Yang and the foundation of the acquired constitution because it is the resource of the reproduction of *qi* and blood. The Spleen *qi* is in charge of sending up essential substances. It functions to digest food and transport nutrients, to control the blood and keep the blood circulating in a normal way, and to nourish the flesh. It has its outward manifestation on the lips and has its specific body opening in the mouth. In the *Ling Shu Ben Shen*, it reads: "Anxiety is the emotional manifestation of the Spleen, as human ideas and thinking are related to the Spleen. It has little blood and abundant *qi*."

Qi and blood flow to the Heart at 11–13 o'clock

The Heart acts as a monarch which governs the mental and emotional activities. The Heart pertains to Fire in the five elements, so it is not good if Fire goes up and covers the Heart. The Heart has the same pronunciation as "new" in Chinese and, being in charge of blood and vessels, it "renews" blood every day. If the renewing is kept without interruption, a human being is in normal health, otherwise he will be ill. The situation of the Heart can be reflected by the pulse and by the face complexion. The Heart opens into the tongue and lies between the Lung and the Pericardium. The pericardiac network connects the Heart with the Lung, Spleen, Stomach, Kidneys, and Bladder. That is why the pericardiac network is considered as the outside defense network of the Heart. The Heart acts as the monarch of the five Zang-organs and six Fu-organs. It belongs to the meridian of Shaoyin. It has little blood and abundant *qi*.

Qi and blood flow to the Small Intestine at 13–15 o'clock

The Small Intestine serves as an organ or place of receiving food from the Stomach and digesting the food. It pertains to Fire in the five elements. It is on the left side of the Stomach, with its upper part connected to the Stomach and its lower part to the Large Intestine and the Urinary Bladder. The Large Intestine and the Urinary Bladder receive respectively solid or liquid substances digested by the Small Intestine. The Spleen functions to transform *qi* which goes up, whereas the Small Intestine functions to transform *qi* which goes down. The Intestine has the same pronunciation in Chinese as "smooth," and accordingly, the Small Intestine functions to make *qi* in the Stomach transport smoothly. A human being is in normal health if the *qi* in the Stomach is transported smoothly, otherwise he is ill. The Small Intestine belongs to the Shaoyang meridian, and it has abundant blood and little *qi*.

Qi and blood flow to the Urinary Bladder at 15–17 o'clock

The Urinary Bladder serves as a local official in charge of a prefecture, and it is where the fluid is restored, *qi* transformed, and water discharged. It pertains to Water in the five elements. Its meridian is connected with the Kidney meridian, and the two meridians are externally–internally related with each other. The Urinary Bladder has the same pronunciation as "bright" in Chinese, because the sufficient original *qi* of *qi* and blood guarantees that fluid reaches everywhere, making the flesh, skin, and hair bright. It belongs to the meridian of Foot-Taiyang and has abundant blood and little *qi*.

Qi and blood flow to the Kidney at 17–19 o'clock

The Kidney acts as an office of promoting strength and health, and it is where skills are created. The Kidney is one of the water Zang-organs. The vital essence and the mind are stored in the Kidney. It is the congenital foundation, vessel for the vital essence and vitality, and the root of life. The Kidney has the same pronunciation as "to lead" in Chinese, which refers to leading *qi* to flow into the bone marrow. It also means "in charge" because it controls the bones, which actually means it is in charge of sexual intercourse and able to make one strong or weak. It dominates the bones; its condition is reflected by the hairs; and it opens into the genitals and anus. It belongs to the Foot-Shaoyin meridian and has little blood and abundant *qi*.

Qi and blood flow to the danzhong (the pericardiac network, also named hand–heart controller) at 19–21 o'clock

The *danzhong* acts as an envoy. It is called the ministerial fire and considered as the outside defense of water Zang-organs. The *danzhong* functions as the representative of the monarch and has the title of the controller. It is connected with the hands to keep the meridian of Jueyin in good condition. It belongs to the meridian of Pericardium-Hand Three-Yin. The pericardial network and the Pericardium provide a conformable relation between the Hand and the Heart. The Pericardium means that the Heart dominates the five Zang-organs; thus the five Zang-organs plus *danzhong* amount to six Zang-organs in total. The *danzhong* belongs to the Hand meridian of Jueyin and the Foot collateral and has abundant blood and little *qi*.

Qi and blood flow to the Triple Energizer at 21–23 o'clock

The Triple Energizer (Sanjiao) serves as an official who deals with the three excess syndromes, and it is where the water course starts. Jiao means "hot" in Chinese, and Triple refers to the *qi* of all the Upper Jiao, the Middle Jiao, and the Lower Jiao. Only if the heat filling the cavity is well dispersed and adequate protection provided can the water course be barrier-free. The water will flow upward if the Upper Jiao is out of control; the water will remain in the middle cavity if the Middle Jiao is out of control; and bowel movements and urination will be disturbed if the Lower Jiao is in disorder. The meridians and collaterals will be unimpeded and the water course is barrier-free if the *qi* of the Triple Energizer is well under control. That is why the Triple Energizer is called the official who deals with the three excess syndromes. It belongs to the meridian of Shaoyang and has little blood and abundant *qi*.

D. GUIDE TO POINT STRIKING

1. Cut arteries

Movements: *B* steps forward with the right foot and delivers a right-hand punch to *A*'s chest. *A* uses the left hand to block *B*'s right fist to the side and then quickly steps forward with the right foot and chops the carotid artery on *B*'s neck by using the knife-edge of the open right hand. (Figures 11.1–11.3)

FIGURE 11.1

FIGURE 11.2

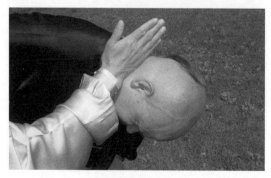

FIGURE 11.3

2. Two dragons take pearls (jab the eyes)

Movements: *B* steps forward with the right foot and delivers a right-hand punch to *A*'s chest. *A* uses the left hand to block *B*'s right fist to the side and then quickly steps forward with the right foot and uses the index and middle fingers of the right hand to jab *B* in the eyes. (Figures 11.4–11.6)

FIGURE 11.4

FIGURE 11.5

FIGURE 11.6

3. Hit the danzhong

Movements: *B* steps forward with the left foot and delivers a left-hand punch towards *A*'s face. *A* uses the right hand to block *B*'s left fist to the side, neutralizing *B*'s punch. *A* then quickly steps forward with the left foot and uses the right hand to punch *B* at the *danzhong* acupoint at the pit of the stomach area. (Figures 11.7–11.9)

FIGURE 11.7

FIGURE 11.8

FIGURE 11.9

4. Zhuihun palm

Movements: *B* steps forward with the right foot and delivers a right-hand punch to *A*'s chest. *A* uses the left hand to block *B*'s right fist to the side. *A* then quickly steps forward and around *B* to *B*'s back right side and strikes *B* to the back of the head with the palm of the right hand. (Figures 11.10–11.12)

FIGURE 11.10

FIGURE 11.11

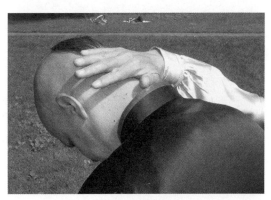

FIGURE 11.12

5. Hit the tinggong (ears)

Movements: *B* steps forward with the left foot and delivers a left-hand punch towards *A*'s face. *A* uses the right hand to block *B*'s left fist to the side and then quickly steps forward with the right foot and at the same time uses both hands to slap *B*'s ears. (Figures 11.13–11.15)

FIGURE 11.13

FIGURE 11.14

FIGURE 11.15

6. Jab the zhangmen

Movements: *B* steps forward with the right foot and delivers a right-hand punch to *A*'s chest. *A* uses the right hand to block *B*'s right fist to the side and then quickly steps forward with the left foot and uses the index finger of the left hand to jab *B* at the *zhangmen* acupoint. (Figures 11.16–11.18)

FIGURE 11.16

FIGURE 11.17

FIGURE 11.18

7. Jab the danshen

Movements: *B* steps forward with the right foot and delivers a right-hand punch to *A*'s chest. *A* uses the right hand to block *B*'s right fist to the side and then quickly steps forward with the right foot and uses the point of the right elbow to strike *B* at the kidneys. (Figures 11.19–11.21)

FIGURE 11.19

FIGURE 11.20

FIGURE 11.21

E. TIME PERIOD CHART OF POINT STRIKING

Period of day (o'clock)	Flourishing meridian	Flowing situation of *qi* and blood	Secrets for relief of injury	Striking point	Closing point
Zi (23–1)	Gallbladder (GBM)	Region below xiphoid, connecting with GBM	Quanjing	Renzhong, connecting with LRM	Ankle, connecting with SJM
Chou (1–3)	Liver (LRM)	Quanjing (Tanzhong)	Jingkou	Tianting (forehead), connecting with LUM	Waist, connecting with GBM
Yin (3–5)	Lung (LUM)	Jingkou (nostril), connecting with LUM	Shangen (root of nose)	Qiaokong (nose bridge), connecting with LIM	Eye, connecting with LIM
Mao (5–7)	Large Intestine (LIM)	Shangen, connecting with LIM	Teeth and cheek	Teeth and cheek, connecting with STM	Face, connecting with LUM
Chen (7–9)	Stomach (STM)	Tianxin (Baihui), connecting with DUM	Fengtou (Yuzhen)	Shuangyin (left and right Taiyang), connecting with BLM	Head, connecting with LIM
Si (9–11)	Spleen (SPM)	Fengtou, connecting with DUM	Zhongyuan	Jiangtai (Shangcang)	Hand, connecting with STM
Wu (11–13)	Heart (HTM)	Zhongyuan (Mingmen), connecting with KIM	Changong (Shenshu)	Wrist pulse	Chest, connecting with SPM
Wei (13–15)	Small Intestine (SIM)	Changong	Fengwei (Changqiang)	Qikan	Abdomen, connecting with HTM
Shen (15–17)	Bladder (BLM)	Fengwei, connecting with RNM	Qujing	Dantian, connecting with KIM	Heart, connecting with SIM

Period of day (o'clock)	Flourishing meridian	Flowing situation of *qi* and blood	Secrets for relief of injury	Striking point	Closing point
You (17–19)	Kidney (KIM)	Qujing, connecting with RNM	Danshen	Baihai (Beihai)	Kidney, connecting with BLM
Xu (19–21)	Pericardium (PCM)	Danshen (Guanyuan), connecting with RNM	Liugong (Pubis)	Penis, connecting with RNM	Neck, connecting with KIM
Hai (21–23)	Sanjiao (SJM)	Liugong, connecting with RNM	Region below xiphoid	Yongquan	Thigh, connecting with PCM and GBM

Analysis:

- Points open as denoted by Midday–Midnight Point Selection
- Strike a point one period prior to its opening time to defeat the opponent when *qi* and blood at the point are to flourish
- Strike a point one period after it opens to defeat the opponent when *qi* and blood at the point are declined

CHAPTER XII

A Few Stories about Masters

A. GRANDMASTER CHEN FAKE

1. Contest with Master Xu Yusheng

Grandmaster Chen Fake was born in 1887 and passed away in 1957 at 71 years of age. As the ninth generation successor of Chen-style Taijiquan, he was well known to society because of his martial art standard and highly praised for his virtue and accomplishments.

He came to Beijing to teach Taijiquan in October 1928, and from then on, Chen-style Taijiquan was revealed to the world. Naturally, a number of Yang-style Taijiquan, Baguazhang, and Xingyiquan masters were attracted to test their skills against Grandmaster Chen Fake. Master Xu Yusheng, a famous veteran Taijiquan master, was one of them.

Master Xu had learned from Grandmasters Yang Shaohou and Yang Chengfu. Four photographs of Master Xu playing push-hands with Grandmaster Yang Chengfu were included in a book entitled *Taijiquan* by Chen Weiming, published in 1924 in Shanghai. Master Xu also published a book on Taijiquan by Guan Baiyi (who became a Chen stylist later) in 1910, in which Guan declared that Taijiquan was created by Zhang Sanfeng. Master Xu believed that claim to be true until he had his encounter with Grandmaster Chen Fake.

Master Xu, together with two other martial artists, asked to have a contest with Grandmaster Chen Fake, but Grandmaster Chen refused the request. Master Xu kept pursuing the matter and finally got Chen to agree, albeit reluctantly. The venue for the contest was an area of forty square yards and it was surrounded by spectators.

After the two competitors entered the area of the contest, Master Xu suddenly attacked Grandmaster Chen vigorously, but, to Xu's surprise, a powerful force came back at him. The force was so powerful that Master Xu was thrown out of the ring of spectators, causing some spectators to fall to the ground as well. The most marvelous thing was that no one had clearly seen how Grandmaster Chen attacked back. Master Xu could not help admiring Grandmaster Chen Fake's profound internal energy and later became his disciple.

2. Two or three movements enough to decide victory or defeat

Afterwards, Master Xu Yusheng took charge of a martial arts competition and invited Grandmaster Chen Fake to be a special adviser. Master Xu showed great respect to Grandmaster Chen and often consulted him.

One day the advisers met and tried to decide how long the rounds of the competition should be. Someone suggested a maximum of fifteen minutes. However, Grandmaster Chen Fake believed that fifteen minutes was much more than needed. He thought that three minutes would be more than enough and, among skilled players, the winner or loser could be decided in the first two or three movements.

Master Li Jianhua, a coach of martial arts and Baguazhang at the Northeast University and also one of the special advisers, was against Grandmaster Chen's point of view. Grandmaster Chen said to him smilingly, "If you don't mind, let us do a little practical verification of what I said." Master Li accepted the suggestion.

Master Li Jianhua, a big man standing over two meters tall, moved swiftly at Grandmaster Chen Fake. As he tried to strike Grandmaster Chen on the chest with his palm, Chen's body moved only a little bit and Master Xu was thrown against a wall and fell down. The paint on the wall flaked off because of the impact. All the people at the scene were shocked.

Master Li stood up. "Now I am convinced. Three minutes will be more than enough," he said loudly to Grandmaster Chen, and continued by examining himself, saying, "I think I was injured." Grandmaster Chen calmly asked, "Injured where?" After further inspection, Master Li found that he was not in the slightest degree injured.

Master Li told the others that powder from the wall paint had embedded so deeply into the fabric of his robe that he could not remove it even by a brush. All the people admired Grandmaster Chen's high standard of Taijiquan *gongfu* in controlling his internal energy, and they often consulted him from then on. Also, Master Li became one of Grandmaster Chen Fake's disciples soon afterwards.

3. A contest between Taiji and wrestling

Master Shen Yousan, also called Shen San (the third) as he was the third son in the family, was a top-grade wrestler. An energetic, middle-sized man, he was famous for his high technical skill, fast and dexterous movements, and tendency to assume airs. He earned his living by performing wrestling in the Tian Qiao area of Beijing and selling medical herbs.

One day, Master Shen Yousan met with Grandmaster Chen Fake. After expressing their respect to one another, Master Shen said that wrestlers did not understand what Taijiquan was or what functions it had as it looked slow and soft and more like dance than a martial art. "What would happen in a match between a wrestling master and a Taijiquan master?" he asked. "It would be very interesting, I guess. A Taijiquan master should be able to meet any master of any school of martial arts, just like Grandmaster Yang Luchan who was known as Yang the Invincible. However, I am not as good as him," Grandmaster Chen replied, smiling.

Master Shen then asked for a trial. Grandmaster Chen stretched out both arms and asked Master Shen to grasp them. Master Shen grasped Grandmaster Chen's arms. Seconds later, the two were laughing and the trial contest seemed to be over even before it had started. What the other people saw was the two sides moving their positions slightly for about five seconds.

Two days later, when Grandmaster Chen Fake was teaching Taijiquan at the Residence of Henan Native Society in Xuanwu District, Master Shen paid a visit to Grandmaster Chen, carrying gifts. He greeted Grandmaster Chen and expressed his thanks. "Not at all," Grandmaster Chen simply said.

Grandmaster Chen's disciples were confused as they did not know what the two masters were talking about. Master Shen noticed the students' confusion and asked them, "Didn't your master tell you what happened between us?"; to this everyone answered, "No, he didn't," or, "We don't know what happened."

"Your master is extraordinary!" Master Shen exclaimed in admiration. He was so excited that he slapped his own thighs and made a thumbs-up gesture. "He is extraordinary for not only his superb *gongfu*, but also his first-class virtue. Everyone believed nothing happened during our contest. Actually, we probed and learned each other's skill level immediately when we started. As I held his arms, I tried to borrow his force for employing my force. However, I found nothing to borrow. Then I released my own force, but it bounced back and my techniques proved useless. To try to throw him, I had to grasp him first. It's unbelievable that an internal energy always emitted from his arms or body wherever I grasped and my fingers were almost injured sometimes. His body was there, but seemed not to be there according to my feeling. As a last resort, I tried to wrestle him to the ground, but that failed as well, like an ant trying to topple a giant tree. His *gongfu*, I knew, was much better than mine. He could have thrown me off, but to save my face he didn't. He hasn't bragged afterwards about what he did either. He is a real friend of mine, I should say. Today, I have come specially to extend my respect."

4. Grandmaster Chen Fake respected both himself and the others

After Master Shen San left, the disciples asked Grandmaster Chen why he did not throw Master Shen off. "Why should I throw him off for nothing? Would you like to be thrown off if you were in the same position as him?" Grandmaster Chen said seriously. "It is difficult for a martial artist to come to fame. We should treasure and respect their fame. A real martial artist never destroys others' fame for his own interests."

Grandmaster Chen Fake never challenged others. He accepted a challenge only if he was repeatedly requested. When he accepted a challenge, he always told the opponent, "You may do your best to attack me. I won't do any injury to you and won't blame you if I am injured."

He never caused anybody an injury and asked his disciples and students to act likewise. He was respected and highly praised by martial artists of each school of martial arts in all the twenty-nine years that he lived in Beijing. This was extraordinary because at that time martial artists were inclined to look down on each other and competition between them was fierce.

Once, Grandmaster Chen was invited as a martial arts coach and offered a very good salary by a private university. However, he politely refused the position when he learned that the authority of the university was planning to dismiss the current coach and the university could not afford to have two coaches at the same time. Actions like this brought him the highest reputation.

B. GRANDMASTER HU YAOZHEN

Once on the fifth day of the Chinese New Year, Feng Zhiqiang together with more than ten other disciples paid Grandmaster Hu Yaozhen, their master, a New Year's call. Grandmaster Hu was delighted to see so many disciples. While they were chatting pleasantly, Grandmaster Hu said to his disciples, "Now, I am going to show you the effect of standing pole (*zhan zhuang*) exercises."

After leading the disciples to the yard, he assumed a standing pole posture. Then he asked two disciples to hold his left arm and another two to hold his right arm, and then ordered them all to pull him forward forcefully. At the same time, he arranged two disciples to push him on the back. Astonishingly, Grandmaster Hu, despite being dragged forcefully by six strong young men, remained unmoved like an iron pagoda. Suddenly, Grandmaster Hu made a movement called "Golden Rooster Shakes Its Feathers" and all six men were shaken immediately to the ground.

After that, Grandmaster Hu asked a disciple to punch him in the abdomen (*dantian* region). When the disciple attacked with a strong punch, Grandmaster Hu did not move his hands at all but only countered with a *neigong* (internal exercise/skill) technique called *dantian* surge. The disciple fell back five or six meters.

According to Grandmaster Feng Zhiqiang's recollection, the disciples were so shocked that they were afraid of being chosen as the next one to strike Grandmaster Hu. They hid behind the columns or corners of the house and some even fled to the inside of the house and peered out from the window, even though they all had been eagerly looking forward to seeing their master's top-grade *neigong* demonstrated.

"Today I gave you a demonstration of *neigong* in order to let you understand the importance of cultivating *neigong*," Grandmaster Hu said earnestly to the disciples at the dinner table that evening. "The cultivation of *neigong* is as important as the foundation of a house," he said. While speaking, he took a chopstick and pitched it out toward the door. The chopstick flew like an arrow and sank halfway into the wooden door.

While the disciples were still stunned by what they witnessed, Grandmaster Hu continued, "As you have all seen today, the proverb that goes 'One will obtain nothing if one practices martial arts without exercising *gong*' is something you should all remember. I hope you attach great importance to practicing *gong*. When your *neigong* is good enough, you can not only enjoy health and longevity, but also gain the ability to manipulate acupoints and give massage therapy in Chinese traditional medicine. With good *neigong*, you will also be able to use hard Qigong to break bricks or stones with a palm, be more powerful and energetic in form play or competition, be more overwhelming in using weapons, and be more effective in utilizing fighting techniques."

The disciples were convinced by what Grandmaster Hu said. They decided to practice *neigong* diligently.

C. GRANDMASTER FENG ZHIQIANG, THE "GIANT OF TAIJI"

1. Power exceeding one thousand pounds

During the 1960s, Master Feng Zhiqiang worked at the Beijing General Factory of Electromotor. One day, when he was working nearby, there was a sudden abnormal noise coming from a core of an electromotor being carried by a crane in the workshop. The core was escaping from the crane rope. Master Feng, noticing the danger, made a sudden big stride forward and caught the huge falling thing.

All the people at the scene were shocked by what Master Feng did. The electromotor core weighed 1100 pounds. To lift that sort of weight, seven or eight strong young men would need to work hard together. More and more employees heard the story, and among them were some young people who, out of curiosity, tried to pursue Master Feng to show his *gongfu*. They even bullied him to provoke him into action, but he always smiled in return and refused to show them anything.

There was an amateur wrestling team composed of twelve strong and vigorous young men at that time in the factory. One day when Master Feng was passing by their training ground, the wrestlers saw him. They gathered around him and asked for a fight.

Master Feng could not refuse this time. "You can line up and push me then," he said.

The young wrestlers then lined up in single file like the carriages of a train and the first one at the head of the line put both hands on Master Feng's abdomen. Following a "1...2...3...push!" all twelve young men pushed forward, exerting themselves to the utmost. Master Feng descended his body, rotated his *dantian*, and made the whole line of young men fall to the ground.

2. Punishing thugs and stopping a robbery

One day when Master Feng was on his way home from work, he heard somebody crying. He went closer and saw that three thugs were trying to steal a bicycle from a girl.

Shouting "Mind your own business!" each thug pulled out a knife, staring at and threatening Master Feng. "Witnessing this makes it my business," Master Feng said angrily, and promptly knocked one of them out. Another one stabbed fiercely at Master Feng, but Master Feng made a sudden dodge to the side, grabbed hold of the attacker's wrist, and knocked the knife down to the ground. The last thug dashed toward Master Feng from his back. Feng dropped down and threw the attacker over his shoulder.

The three thugs ended up being so threatened that they ran away. Master Feng accompanied the girl to her home. When the girl was about to thank Master Feng, he had already disappeared into the darkness.

3. Defeating a strong American

A veteran worker came to the physical therapy room on the campus of the Beijing Sports College (Beijing University of Sports) on September 2, 1981. The man looked very strong, with thick eyebrows and big eyes. He was Master Feng, who was invited there as a massage therapist.

A short while later, martial arts coach Men Huifeng came, accompanied by a strong American man. The American came there every day to have massage therapy. In fact, he did not come for medical service, but to learn Chinese massage technique.

After the massage, the therapist, called Li, asked the American, "Don't you want to meet Master Feng?" The American was surprised: "Master who?"

"Master Feng Zhiqiang," Li smiled.

The strong American was the coach of the American Research Society of Martial Arts. He was thirty-three years old and over 1.8 meters tall. He weighed more than ninety kilos. Also, he was a Judo gold medalist in America. He started to practice Monkey boxing and Shaolin boxing when he was six years old, and later Aikido, Xingyi, Bagua, and Taijiquan. He had visited more than fifty countries, including India, where he spent two years learning Yoga.

Before China, he had visited Southeast Asia and Hong Kong and had not found his match. Being enormously proud of his success, the American had come to visit Beijing Sports College and had sought out several Taijiquan and Xingyi practitioners with whom he had tested his skills. "I won't meet with people like them any more. It's a waste of time," he said in dissatisfaction.

As for Master Feng Zhiqiang, he first learnt Tongbei boxing from Han Xiaofeng who came from Cangzhou. Next he learnt Liuhexinyi and Taoist Qigong from Hu Yaozhen who came from Shanxi province. In 1951, he started to learn Chen-style Taijiquan from the famous Chen Fake who came from Chen Village of Henan Province. Feng was taught the essence of the techniques of Chen-style Taijiquan and he could be said to be Grandmaster Chen Fake's most brilliant disciple. He had competed with martial artists specialized in Tongbei boxing, Paochui, Xingyi, Bagua, and wrestling and obtained their admiration for his *gongfu* and virtue.

After the initial greetings, the American performed several postures and hand techniques of Monkey boxing. "What do you think?" he asked.

"Your upper body was powerful, whereas your lower body looked unstable," commented Master Feng.

The American certainly was not convinced. He "modestly" invited Master Feng to show some hand techniques. "All right, you attack and I will deal with it then," Grandmaster Feng said.

The strong American was extremely glad. Using his full strength, he charged at Master Feng like a hungry tiger. Master Feng raised both his arms to meet the attack. He quickly dropped his shoulders and elbows and moved his left knee between the American's legs. In Taijiquan terms, Feng's movements would be "Guide the opponent to enter into emptiness."

Feeling that he had met nothing and that he was leaning forward, the American immediately withdrew to regain balance. However, with Master Feng's right knee blocking his left knee, he could not keep his balance. Master Feng tapped his chest to distract him, and then explosively emitted force with both hands. Before reacting, the American was tossed backward. The result might have been serious if there had not been some people preventing him from falling to the ground.

"Master Feng, you are extremely good. Extremely good," the American praised in less-than-perfect Chinese while making a thumbs-up gesture.

Modestly, Master Feng showed his little finger and said, "I am like this in China. There are many who are better than me."

4. Chen-style Taijiquan returning home

Chen Village in Wen County, Henan Province, is the birthplace of Chen-style Taijiquan where grandmasters have risen in every generation. Grandmaster Chen Fake was the representative of the ninth generation as his *gongfu* was considered the best.

In 1928, Grandmaster Chen Fake left Chen Village for Peiping (Beijing), where he settled down and started to teach Chen-style Taijiquan. Starting from that time, Beijing became the center of Chen-style Taijiquan.

In 1976, the "Cultural Revolution" ended, and it was like the coming of spring when nature comes back to life. Chinese Wushu and other traditional cultures started to regain vigor. A campaign for the systematic preservation of traditional Wushu was launched nationwide. However, people in Chen

Village were in difficulty, as Taijiquan in the village had been seriously affected during the Cultural Revolution.

An invitation from Chen Village reached Grandmaster Feng Zhiqiang. It was written by Zhang Weizhen, the secretary of the Communist Party of the village. Zhang, representing all the people in the village, earnestly and sincerely invited Grandmaster Feng to Chen Village to teach Taijiquan.

Later, the secretary came to Beijing together with Master Wang Xian, the deputy secretary and principal of Chen Village Wushu College, and they visited Feng to reaffirm the invitation in person. Mr. Chen Boxian and Mr. Chen Xiaowang, eleventh generation successors of Chen-style Taijiquan, came to Beijing as well, in order to accompany Grandmaster Feng to Chen Village.

Grandmaster Feng felt the trust the villagers put in him. Recalling how Grandmaster Chen Fake trained him and entrusted him to develop Chen-style Taijiquan, he accepted the invitation. He paid three visits to the village and passed on all he had learned from the grandmaster to the martial artists of the eleventh generation. He taught them the Taoist standing post, among other exercises. From then on, this important *neigong* exercise was added to the curriculum of Chen-style Taijiquan.

Also, the people of Chen Village often visited Grandmaster Feng for advanced training. It was always pleasing and a relief to Grandmaster Feng to witness that Chen-style Taijiquan was flourishing.

5. Shanghai astonished by genuine Taiji

The National Joint Performance by Prominent Masters was held in Shanghai in July 1982. At that time, there was a surge of interest in Taiji in the metropolitan martial arts circles.

Master Feng became one of the hottest names during the surge. People wanted to see the elegant demeanor of the highest representative of Chen stylists, famous for his victory over a foreign martial artist. In the National Joint Performance event, all martial artists were to perform push-hands with their own disciples except Master Feng. He was to demonstrate push-hands with martial artists chosen by the organizer of the event.

In the first section of the performance, the organizing committee selected a Taijiquan practitioner as Master Feng's opponent. No sooner had the opponent touched hands with Master Feng than he was thrown off— thrown off so far away that he bumped heavily against the rostrum and knocked teacups down from the table there.

Another opponent was designated for Master Feng's push-hands performance in the second section. The opponent, a skilled practitioner of external-style (*waijia*) *gongfu* and hard Qigong, was very famous for showing little mercy to his opponents. When the demonstration started, the opponent launched an attack with all his strength. Master Feng simply used a movement called "Yellow Dragon Stirs Water Three Times" and threw him to the ground. Later Master Feng made him fall down to the ground employing the technique of "Guide the opponent to enter into emptiness."

Master Feng's superb skills made the participants and the spectators breathless with admiration. Even the opponent admired Master Feng from the bottom of his heart. He said aloud what everyone was already thinking: "Master Feng's *gongfu* is real *gongfu*. Master Feng's Taijiquan is real Taijiquan."

During the event, Master Feng and his real Taijiquan became a hot topic within the martial arts community in Shanghai.

6. At the gathering of prominent figures in Beijing

After national push-hands competitions were resumed in 1982, several competitions had been held. However, at the competitions, most competitors often bulldozed each other, as their technique, generally speaking, was not very advanced. They did not compete in the Taijiquan style. Some people even started to doubt the applicability of the techniques described in the classics of Taijiquan. To tackle this problem, China Wushu Research Institute decided to host a national workshop on Taijiquan push-hands.

The workshop opened at a training center run by the China Wushu Academy in a suburb of Beijing in 1990. Prominent representatives of each style and champions of various competitions were invited to participate in the workshop. At the workshop, some people believed that some of the rules of the contest restricted the application of techniques, whereas some others complained that the small area made the competitors bulldoze or drag each other in contest.

As for Master Feng Zhiqiang, representative of Chen-style Taijiquan, he believed that it was the competitors' low standard of *gongfu* that caused the bulldozing and dragging in competitions. Consequently, the promotion of competitors' level of *gongfu* and techniques was the most effective way to tackle the bulldozing problem.

Following the agenda, during the practice of push-hands, the champions of various weight classes were invited to do push-hands, and the experts were invited to provide technical instructions whenever problems emerged.

Naturally, Master Feng, among the prominent martial artists, acted as a major instructor.

When two competitors got in a bull–bull fight, Master Feng intervened. He pointed out that they were deadlocked because neither side dared to relax and, at this moment, one side should do so in order to "Guide the opponent to enter into emptiness" for neutralizing the opponent's energy.

Then Master Feng, in his sixties, personally did push-hands with them and showed them how to prevent the bull–bull fight effectively. He demonstrated two situations. First, when the opponent grasped his arms and pushed with great strength, he moved his arms backward to lead the opponent, and then quickly sprang them forward to throw the opponent off as the opponent's force was used and the opponent had yet to generate new force. Second, when the opponent gave him a push on the chest using their full strength, he just turned from the waist to neutralize the opponent's force, and then quickly stepped out, emitted force, and threw the opponent off as the opponent lost balance; when the opponent stood up and grasped his arms and pushed once more, he employed the technique of "interchange between yin and yang" to neutralize the opponent's force and strike the opponent down quickly.

Master Feng's personal demonstration as well as verbal instruction was convincing and the competitors decided to spend more time and energy improving their techniques.

7. Teacher of famous persons

At the farewell banquet of the National Taiji Push-hands Workshop, the representative of Henan Province, Master Zhang Maozhen, poured wine for the leaders of the National Wushu Research Institute, eminent representatives, and martial art champions. "I was born in a family with Wushu tradition. I have engaged in *gongfu* for decades and won some reputation in Zhengzhou City and elsewhere in Henan Province. At this workshop, however, after having witnessed Master Feng Zhiqiang's performance, I deeply feel that the pursuit of Wushu is endless. I very much admire Master Feng and would like to take him as my Wushu master and relearn Taijiquan from now on. All the leaders and friends at the banquet are kindly invited to testify my heartfelt hope," he said excitedly.

Very soon after he said that, Mr. Cao Zhilin stood up. "I have practiced Wushu for twenty years and devoted a lot of time and energy to push-hands. I won championships in the sixty-five kilos weight class in the Shanghai Push-hands Competition in 1982 and 1986 and in the National

Push-hands Competition in 1986. I know Taijiquan enables 'the weak to defeat the strong,' 'adhere/connect/stick/follow,' 'neither separating nor fighting force head-on,' 'guide the opponent to enter into emptiness,' 'use four ounces to deflect one thousand pounds,' and 'win with ingenuity.' However, in fact, win-by-preponderance has been unavoidable for me in push-hands practice. Having learnt push-hands and fighting technique as well as Hunyuan Qigong from Master Feng, I got the secret. Especially, when I saw the techniques Master Feng showed several times, I deeply understood what profound art Taijiquan was. So, I want to be one of Master Feng's disciples in order to further promote my level of push-hands and skill in fighting," he said.

Enthusiastic applause echoed as they spoke. A toast was proposed to Master Feng and his two "disciples."

D. MASTER WANG FENGMING, THE "KING OF NEIGONG"

1. Skill of point striking

Following a recommendation, a man came to Beijing to visit Master Wang Fengming. Talking with the visitor, Master Wang learned that the visitor's name was Li and that he was a detective with the Public Security Bureau of Hunan Province. Mr. Li was very fond of Wushu. He was a gold medal winner of free fighting at provincial competitions. He had also been awarded many times for his good service as he had often subdued suspects who were committing physical assault or murder.

After talking for a while, Mr. Li changed the topic by saying that he wanted to test Master Wang's skills. When he and Master Wang extended their arms and touched hands, he felt that his arms were stuck with glue and his body bound with ropes. He could not get rid of the contact no matter what methods he used or efforts he made. He was totally confused and asked Master Wang, "What kind of technique are you using?"

"The 'adhere/connect/stick/follow' technique of Taijiquan," Master Wang replied.

"Would you mind if I used free-fighting methods?" Mr. Li then asked.

"Go ahead!" Master Wang agreed without any hesitation.

This time, Mr. Li fully used his free-fighting skills. With his right fist, he tried to strike Master Wang a quick and powerful blow on the chest—a technique called "Black Tiger Hits the Heart." Master Wang deflected the incoming fist with his left hand, stepped forward and put his right leg behind Mr. Li's right leg, and then put his right arm against Mr. Li's neck. Master Wang moved very quickly and used the "Lotus Kick" of Taijiquan, throwing Mr. Li to the ground.

The free-fighting champion got back on his legs quickly and tried to strike Master Wang to the face. Master Wang made a sudden dodge to the side and diverted the fist with his right hand. When Mr. Li's ribs were exposed, Master Wang stepped in and directed *qi* to two fingers of his left hand, which he then used to strike Mr. Li at the *zhangmen* acupoint.

The strike was so painful that Mr. Li had to bend and squat down with his hands on his ribs as if he had been stabbed with a sword. He opened his mouth but could not breathe, and his face turned pale. Noticing his suffering, Master Wang massaged several acupoints on his body, and a little while later, Mr. Li made a long exhalation and recovered to normal.

All those who have experienced Master Wang's point-striking art tend to be filled with admiration. Mr. Li is one of them and became one of Master Wang's disciples.

2. Defeating a Japanese fighter three times

a. Unannounced attack

In 1990, Master Wang Fengming and Grandmaster Feng Zhiqiang visited Tokyo, Japan, to teach Taijiquan at the invitation of the Japan–China Taijiquan Exchange Society. One day when Master Wang was leading form practice, he suddenly felt a powerful strike in his back. Master Wang quickly turned his body, held the attacker's hand, and diverted the attack, following the attacker's movement. As a result, the attacker fell down. The trainees were surprised and did not know what had happened.

"Attacking me like that was not very polite," Master Wang said to the man with the help of an interpreter.

The man managed to stand up and make a deep bow. "I am sorry, Mr. Wang. It was impolite," he said.

After class, some of the trainees told Master Wang the name of the man. They also told him that the man had practiced karate and judo and that he, as a beginner in Taijiquan, wanted to know how Taijiquan techniques are used in fighting and how good Master Wang's *gongfu* would be.

The workshop was concluded. Before Grandmaster Feng Zhiqiang and Master Wang Fengming left for China, Mr. Koike Tsutomu, who was in charge of the Japan–China Taijiquan Exchange Society, approached Master Wang and invited him to stay in Japan and teach Taijiquan for a year. When

Master Wang politely refused the request because of the tight schedule he had in China, Mr. Koike invited him immediately to pay another visit to Japan and teach Taijiquan the following year. Apart from these invitations, Master Wang was also invited as an adviser to the Japan–China Taijiquan Exchange Society.

b. Face-to-face contest

At the invitation of the Japan–China Taijiquan Exchange Society, Master Wang Fengming visited Japan a second time in 1991. When Master Wang taught Taijiquan in Tokyo, the man who had attacked him the previous time came there again and took part in the classes.

One day, Master Wang was introducing the main points of the martial application of a movement called "Punch of Draping over Body" and explaining that the movement is often used when the front of one's clothing is being grasped by the opponent. "The technique of gripping the front of the clothes is especially developed in our Judo. One can do nothing to deal with the hold," the previous year's attacker said, and continued, "May we try this movement in practice to see how it goes?"

He immediately came closer and took a tight grip of the front of Master Wang's jacket as soon as Master Wang agreed. With his right hand, Master Wang grasped the man's right wrist, put his left elbow on the man's right elbow joint, and then turned from the waist with elbows conformed to the movement and *qi* mobilized, using the "cutting energy" of Taijiquan. The man fell heavily.

The man tried again with a similar outcome. He then tried gripping with his left hand, but lost once more. Finally, Master Wang allowed the man to hold with both hands and still the result was unchanged. After several attempts, the man could not come up with anything else and had to give up.

c. Sincere admission of defeat

In 1992, Master Wang visited Tokyo a third time to teach Taijiquan. Again, the same man, familiar from previous visits, took part in the training course.

During a class, while he was learning the movements of Taiji push-hands, he found an opportunity to use his skills. He held Master Wang's arms and pushed forcefully. Master Wang first got rid of the arm lock by rotating his wrists and spiraling his arms, and then seized the man's wrists and used the plucking technique, following the man's pushing movement, to "guide the opponent to enter into emptiness." At this moment, the man felt as if he were falling into a bottomless abyss. At the very moment when the man was unbalanced, Master Wang quickly followed and used explosive force. The man was thrown off like a bullet.

The man changed to the seizing and joint-locking technique. He held Master Wang's right wrist with his right hand. Master Wang utilized silk-reeling leading to a counter-hold. The man could not bear the pain that felt as if he were being bitten by a pair of pincers and that his bones and tendons would be broken. He therefore patted three times on the floor.

After three encounters, he was now sincerely convinced. "I used not to value Taijiquan as a fighting art. However, after having participated in Master Wang's training courses of Taijiquan and push-hands in the last three years, I have changed my view," the man said at the farewell banquet. "Now, I am entirely convinced of the unique techniques of 'pitting the small against the big; guiding the opponent to enter into emptiness; deflecting one thousand pounds with four ounces; and ingeniously gaining victory' in Taijiquan."

3. Martial use of the dantian

"Taijiquan belongs to the internal school of martial arts. It is an exercise of mind/intent and *qi*. That's why a practitioner should concentrate on the *dantian*. When cultivating the *dantian* has reached a certain level, a quality of 'when mind/intent arrives, *qi* arrives and movement arrives' can be achieved. Another result of *dantian* cultivation is the ability to directly use the *dantian* in fighting techniques such as seizing and joint-locking," Master Wang told the students during a Taijiquan class on the campus of TSL Adult University in Helsinki.

A trainee was puzzled by Master Wang's words. "I have studied Taijiquan before but have never heard about those functions of the *dantian*. Could you show me, in practice, the usage of the *dantian* in fighting techniques?" he said.

Master Wang first asked the trainee to push him on the *dantian* with both hands. With the trainee pushing, he lowered his center of gravity, lowered *qi* to the *dantian*, and, using a technique called "*dantian* surging," threw the trainee off. The trainee tried once more and the result was the same. Next, the trainee pushed Master Wang on the *dantian* vigorously with his right palm. This time, Master Wang used a method called "*dantian* rotation" to seize and apply a joint lock to the trainee's hand. The trainee cried out in pain, shaking his hand and stamping his feet. "I really didn't think it would be that powerful!" he exclaimed.

"I've practiced Taijiquan for years but made only little progress because I've been stuck doing external movements. It is an honor to know Master Wang, and I believe I have now found a good way to cultivate both Taijiquan and Qigong at the same time," he said to the others after the class.

The editor-in-chief of the *Way*, a magazine in France, interviewed Master Wang and tested in person his unique skills of *dantian* surging and *dantian* rotation during a training course held in Paris in 1996. "As the editor-in-chief of the *Way* magazine in France, I have interviewed many eminent figures in the martial arts world but I've seldom met anyone with Master Wang's level of *neigong*," he said to the public.

4. Example of a skilled victory

Master Wang was practicing Taijiquan forms at the Temple of Heaven one Sunday morning. A foreigner approached him and made a self-introduction in Chinese.

The foreigner was from Saint Petersburg in Russia. He had been interested in martial arts since childhood and had practiced Judo, Karate, Xingyi, and Taijiquan. He had been looking forward to learning Wushu in China one day, and his dream finally came true when the cultural exchange between China and Russia started in 1988. He had the opportunity to learn Wushu at the Beijing Sport University.

After chatting for a while, the Russian expressed that he wanted to try some push-hands with Master Wang. He became inwardly surprised as soon as they started. He could not locate the force in Master Wang's body. Sometimes the body, like cotton, felt insubstantial, agile, and changeable following his movements, and sometimes the body felt heavy and steady like an iron pagoda. Experiencing Master Wang's technique of hardness and softness in coordination with each other, he found no opportunities to exploit, though he was taller and physically stronger than Master Wang.

He therefore changed tactics and grabbed both of Master Wang's arms using his hands and at the same time pushed hard. He felt that one of Master Wang's arms was spiraling backward and his own force just dissipating into nothing. At this moment, Master Wang turned his body and then quickly returned with his hands coordinated with the movement. A beautiful explosive force ensued from Master Wang's movements and the Russian was thrown off.

Learning that holding Master Wang with both hands was not working, the Russian grabbed one of Master Wang's arms with one of his hands and pushed Master Wang on the chest with his other hand. Master Wang turned his body like a revolving door and the Russian's force dissipated into nothing. Then Master Wang, like pushing a boat along with the current, rolled the Russian's arm back and made him fall in one move. Everyone at the scene admired Master Wang's Taiji *gongfu* of pitting the small against the big and winning with ingenious skills.

After crossing hands several times, the Russian was very convinced by Master Wang's superb Taiji *gongfu*. From then on, he came to learn Taijiquan and Qigong from Master Wang at the Temple of Heaven every weekend during his stay in Beijing.

The Russian sent gifts and an invitation to Master Wang when he returned home. He expressed his thanks to Master Wang and invited Master Wang to teach Taijiquan and Qigong in Saint Petersburg. Master Wang politely refused the invitation because his domestic work kept him from going abroad.

Photographs from the Chinese Edition

FOUNDING OF THE CAPITAL WUSHU SOCIETY IN 1953
2nd row, 7th from right: Grandmaster Chen Fake, ninth generation lineage holder of Chen-style Taijiquan, elected as chairman; 2nd row, 8th from right: Grandmaster Hu Yaozhen, prominent lineage holder of Taoist Qigong, elected as vice chairman.

FAMOUS MASTERS FROM EVERY CORNER OF THE COUNTRY
GATHERED AT CHEN VILLAGE, THE ORIGIN OF TAIJIQUAN
1st row, 4th from left: Grandmaster Feng Zhiqiang; 2nd row, 4th from left: Master Wang Fengming.

GRANDMASTER FENG ZHIQIANG DEMONSTRATING
HIS UNIQUE INTERNAL POWER IN 1986

GRANDMASTER FENG ZHIQIANG MEETING WITH MR. WAN LI, CHAIRMAN OF
THE STANDING COMMITTEE OF THE NATIONAL PEOPLE'S CONGRESS, IN 1987

A TRAINING COURSE ORGANIZED BY BEIJING ZHIQIANG WUSHU
ACADEMY IN COOPERATION WITH A DISTRICT PUBLIC SECURITY BRANCH
BUREAU FOR PUBLIC SECURITY PERSONNEL IN BEIJING IN 1988

AS AN EXAMPLE OF "SMALL DEFEATS BIG AND WEAK DEFEATS STRONG," MASTER
WANG FENGMING DOING PUSH-HANDS WITH A RUSSIAN MARTIAL ARTIST IN 1989

GRANDMASTER FENG ZHIQIANG AND HIS DISCIPLE, MASTER WANG
FENGMING, AFTER GIVING A LECTURE IN TOKYO IN 1990

MASTER WANG FENGMING SHOWING EXPLOSIVE ENERGY WHILE DEMONSTRATING
PUSH-HANDS AT THE EUROPEAN TAIJI PUSH-HANDS COMPETITION IN 1993

STUDENTS EXPERIENCING THE SURGES OF INTERNAL *QI* AT THE
DANTIAN DEMONSTRATED BY MASTER WANG FENGMING IN 1994

MASTER WANG FENGMING LEADING HIS STUDENTS' PRACTICE IN FINLAND IN 1995

MASTER WANG FENGMING AND STUDENTS IN PARIS IN 1996

MASTER WANG FENGMING GIVING A LECTURE ON TAIJI
STICK AND RULER QIGONG IN GERMANY IN 1997

GRANDMASTER FENG ZHIQIANG GUIDING TAIJI PUSH-HANDS IN HELSINKI IN 1998

A GROUP PICTURE OF MASTER WANG FENGMING WITH MR. LI LAIREN,
PRINCIPAL OF CANADA CHEN-STYLE TAIJI CULTIVATION COLLEGE, AND
SOME STUDENTS, TAKEN DURING A TEACHING VISIT TO CANADA IN 1999

AT THE THIRD EUROPEAN INTERNATIONAL CHEN-STYLE HUNYUAN
TAIJIQUAN AND QIGONG WORKSHOP HELD IN FINLAND IN 2000

MASTER WANG FENGMING INVITED AS AN HONORABLE DIRECTOR OF ZIBO
CITY ZITONGSHAN WUSHU COLLEGE BY THE DIRECTOR, NI YUANHAI

MASTER WANG FENGMING AND STUDENTS AT THE SIXTH EUROPEAN
INTERNATIONAL CHEN-STYLE HUNYUAN TAIJIQUAN AND QIGONG WORKSHOP IN
SPAIN IN 2003

MASTER WANG FENGMING GIVING A DEMONSTRATION OF SEIZING
AND JOINT-LOCKING SKILLS TO A STUDENT FROM THE USA